New Dawn for the Kissimmee River

T0244009

UNIVERSITY PRESS OF FLORIDA

Florida A&M University, Tallahassee
Florida Atlantic University, Boca Raton
Florida Gulf Coast University, Ft. Myers
Florida International University, Miami
Florida State University, Tallahassee
New College of Florida, Sarasota
University of Central Florida, Orlando
University of Florida, Gainesville
University of North Florida, Jacksonville
University of South Florida, Tampa
University of West Florida, Pensacola

New Dawn for
the Kissimmee River

~~~~~~~~~~~~~~~~~~~~~~~~

Orlando to Okeechobee by Kayak

Doug Alderson

University Press of Florida
Gainesville · Tallahassee · Tampa · Boca Raton
Pensacola · Orlando · Miami · Jacksonville · Ft. Myers · Sarasota

First cloth printing, 2009
First paperback printing, 2024

29   28   27   26   25   24   6   5   4   3   2   1

Library of Congress Cataloging-in-Publication Data
Alderson, Doug.
New dawn for the Kissimmee river: Orlando to Okeechobee by kayak/
Doug Alderson.
p. cm.
Includes bibliographical references and index.
ISBN 978-0-8130-3395-2 (cloth) | ISBN 978-0-8130-8089-5 (pbk.)
1. Kayaking—Florida—Kissimmee River Valley. 2. Kayaking—
Florida—Okeechobee, Lake, Region. 3. Kissimmee River Valley
(Fla.)—Description and travel. 4. Okeechobee, Lake, Region (Fla.)—
Description and travel. I. Title.
GV776.F62K573 2009
797.122'409759539—dc22   2009011116

The University Press of Florida is the scholarly publishing agency
for the State University System of Florida, comprising Florida A&M
University, Florida Atlantic University, Florida Gulf Coast University,
Florida International University, Florida State University, New College
of Florida, University of Central Florida, University of Florida, University of North Florida, University of South Florida, and University of
West Florida.

University Press of Florida
2046 NE Waldo Road
Suite 2100
Gainesville, FL 32609
http://upress.ufl.edu

To Cyndi, for being there for me

Contents

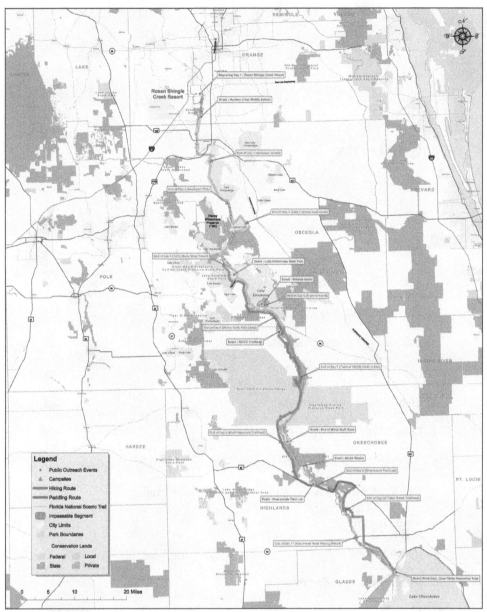

Legend

* Public Outreach Events
△ Campsites
▬▬ Hiking Route
▬▬ Paddling Route
▬▬ Florida National Scenic Trail
▨ Impassable Segment
City Limits
Park Boundaries

Conservation Lands
Federal   Local
State   Private

0   5   10   20 Miles

Expedition Headwaters

**An Everglades
Journey to Remember**
www.dep.state.fl.us/evergladesforeverieh/default.htm

Preface

Merriam-Webster's Collegiate Dictionary defines the word *journey* as "traveling from one place to another; trip." *Journey*, to me, also means discovery and exploration, and all of the surprises, challenges, and encounters with man and beast that go along with it.

The thread throughout this book is a journey—mostly by kayak— from Orlando to Lake Okeechobee through the Kissimmee chain of lakes and the Kissimmee River. For twelve days, my companions and I did not drive a car, sleep in a soft bed, open a refrigerator, check e-mails, or shop at a store other than at a fish camp. Instead, we tuned in to the natural world. We slowed down. We challenged our endurance, coalesced as a team, and coped with hot sun, bugs, and high winds. And we learned about an interconnected band of freshwater that traverses what many are now calling Florida's Heartland, the largest undeveloped chunk of land south of Interstate 4.

The Kissimmee valley—the headwaters and grand gateway to the Everglades—is the domain of the alligator and bald eagle, snail kite and spoonbill. It is a traditional fishing and hunting mecca—the realm of the airboat and john boat—but it's increasingly attracting the attention of outdoor enthusiasts sporting binoculars and kayak paddles. And its long-term health will affect the entire Everglades system and the millions of people who depend upon its freshwater.

The history of the Kissimmee basin is one of reverence, conflict, exploitation, and renewal. The Kissimmee River, once badly damaged by the Army Corps of Engineers in the name of flood control, is now being resurrected in what is regarded as the largest true ecosystem restoration project in the world. We witnessed firsthand, from the perspective of a slow-moving kayak and on foot, the results of those long-term efforts. It gave us hope.

Much of the Kissimmee valley is the home of ranchers, a place where disputes were once settled at gunpoint. Today, conflicts over this land are more internal. Ranchers are increasingly being tempted by lucrative offers from developers and speculators, or they are given a choice to sell land or development rights to the state so the land can remain undeveloped, a haven for many other creatures besides cattle.

Developers are vying for a stake of the Heartland. They seek to build towns on land that had known only grass, palmetto, and trees, and they want roads. The two most notable proposals being put forth are the north-south Heartland Parkway and the east-west Heartland Coast-to-Coast. Whether they are built depends upon the government, market forces, and how much change the general citizenry would like to see regarding the Kissimmee valley and the rest of the Heartland.

Maybe this book will reveal something of what's at stake. Most of these pages are about a journey through a part of Florida few people know, beyond the imaginary worlds of Disney and Orlando. How well it survives in this century and beyond is up to us all.

Acknowledgments

First, I would like to thank those who were part of Expedition Headwaters, both the actual team members and the support people and documentary crew. They are, in alphabetical order: Dale Allen, Deb Blick, Jeff Brooks, Ian Brown, Jeff Cook, Fred Davis, Pete Durnell, Bill Graf, Josh Harris, Doug Hattaway, Terry Johnson, Virginia Johnson, Mike Jones, Beth Kelso, Matt Klein, Vince Matera, Bob Mindick, Ayounga Riddick, Julia Thompson, and Terry Torrens. We were a diverse but compatible group. In the evenings, jokes and funny stories flowed like the waters we paddled. I can't remember when I laughed so much for such an extended period of time.

I'd also like to thank the expedition's sponsors:

Harris Rosen, for dreaming the big dream, and his helpful staff.

The Florida Department of Environmental Protection—especially Jena Brooks, Jim Wood, Heather Pence, and Matt Klein of the Office of Greenways and Trails for asking me to represent the agency, and to Nancy Blum, Vivian Garfein, and Jeff Prather for their public relations efforts. Even though this book was written on my own time, usually from 10 P.M. to midnight or later for several months (ask my wife!), I think it will reflect positively on Florida's efforts to restore the northern Everglades.

The South Florida Water Management District, which provided invaluable support and expertise.

The Florida Trail Association, a blue-ribbon organization that all trail groups could use as a model. The United States Forest Service, which helps to fund the Florida Trail, was also a sponsor.

Bright House Networks and Central Florida News 13, for publicizing the expedition and focusing on the environmental issues of the Kissimmee valley.

Bass Pro Shops, represented by Greg Finenco, and Travel Country Outdoors, represented by Mike Plante, for supplying gear for team members.

The Trust for Public Land, which has enhanced the quality of life for so many.

Osceola County, for all of their support through their geographical domain and beyond.

The folks who helped us along the way also deserve appreciation. They include Joel Noland, the manager of Lake Kissimmee State Park; the staff of the U.S. Air Force Avon Park Bombing Range; the Army Corps of Engineers; Cary Lightsey and the staff of Lightsey Cattle Company on Brahma Island; and Louisa Kerwin of the Riverwoods Field Lab.

I also want to appreciate the good folks at the University Press of Florida for their expertise in bringing this book to print. Thanks to Joe Koebel, senior scientist with the South Florida Water Management District, for reviewing the chapters on the Kissimmee River restoration, and to Bob Mindick, for supplying photos for and feedback on several chapters.

chapter 1

Shingle Creek Beginnings

For a half hour, we were celebrities. Cameras clicked. Crowds cheered. Dignitaries spoke. Television cameras pointed to the seven of us in matching fishing shirts posing in front of our flotilla of kayaks.

We got aboard and paddled around the first bend of the creek. The send-off crowd at the Rosen Shingle Creek Resort disappeared behind us, and we were enveloped by cypress trees that lined the narrow waterway. Great blue herons, snowy egrets, and little blue herons poked along mats of water weeds. Alligators slid quietly beneath the glassy surface. Ospreys cried overhead. It's surprising how quickly one can move in Florida from a busy resort to what seems almost wilderness. Just south of Orlando—home of Disney World, one of the world's most famous resorts—this band of red brown swamp water that is Shingle Creek would carry us to the world's most famous wetlands— the Everglades.

I became involved with Expedition Headwaters as part of my job with the Florida Department of Environmental Protection's Office of Greenways and Trails. My typical duties focused on establishing a sea kayak trail around the entire state—the Florida Circumnavigational Saltwater Paddling Trail. When word got out in January of 2007 that Ayounga Reddick of the South Florida Water Management District, Matt Klein from my office, Bob Mindick of Osceola Parks, and Pete Durnell from the Florida Trail Association were organizing a coalition of public, private, and nonprofit organizations for a twelve-day paddling/hiking expedition from Orlando to Lake Okeechobee in order

Fig. 1. Shingle Creek in the southern part of Orlando—headwaters of the Everglades.

to publicize the plight of the Upper Everglades, I was asked to participate. It didn't take much arm twisting. The idea of paddling 140 miles through the Kissimmee chain of lakes and Kissimmee River without the customary sting of salt water in my eyes was appealing. After two months of coordinating gear, food, overnight stops, and maps for our planned route, our team of seven was ready to begin.

Our paddling route was not a new one. For the Seminoles and native people preceding them, it was a well-traveled waterway. There also were a handful of highly publicized expeditions in the 1800s, but to our knowledge, we would be the first in more than a century to paddle the entire length in one shot. Much of it would be through a surprisingly remote region, and we hoped for good weather. Late March can be a windy time of year in south central Florida, and there is always a chance of severe storms and days of continuous rain. On the plus side, temperatures are normally moderate, and the hurricane season had not yet begun.

I was to take GPS readings at important locations so our route could be used as a future paddling trail, complementing the existing Florida Trail footpath along the Kissimmee River. Other team members would fulfill different roles. Dale Allen and Doug Hattaway of the Trust for Public Land would split time on the trip, gauging the need for more public land purchases along the route that could be used for campsites and land trail corridors. Beth Kelso and Ian Brown of the Florida Trail Association would evaluate hiking potentials. Bob Mindick and Julia Thompson of the Osceola County Parks Division, along with several folks from the South Florida Water Management District and Florida Trail Association, would provide local expertise and logistical support. Mike Jones, retired navy man, would come along as a "private citizen" who simply loved the outdoors.

Bright House Networks, via Rezolution Productions, supplied a film crew that would produce daily television spots for central Florida news programs and an hour-long documentary of the expedition.

Fig. 2. A media crew films the expedition team embarking on Shingle Creek on day one.

Fig. 3. Harris Rosen, one of the trip's sponsors, speaks at the send-off gathering at his Shingle Creek Resort.

Food and equipment would be provided by the Rosen Shingle Creek Resort, Travel County Outdoors, and Bass Pro Shops. Matt Klein of my office was the overall trip coordinator, although he couldn't join us in the field. Everyone involved with the expedition, from the behind-the-scenes folks to those who actually dipped a paddle, contributed special skills and knowledge.

One of the key trip sponsors was a colorful Orlando resort developer—Harris Rosen. At one of our early organizational meetings, he opened his address to a room of mostly government employees this way: "I'm not always convinced that the public sector has the best and brightest," he said. A few folks shifted uncomfortably in their plush chairs, including me. "But I want to let you know," Rosen continued, "how terribly impressive you are. This is a good melding of public and private interests." There was a collective sigh of relief.

After the planning meeting, I chatted with Rosen while leaning on a glassed-in model of his massive resort. "When I purchased this land," said the former hotel planner for Walt Disney, "I didn't realize Shingle Creek even existed until I flew over the property in a helicopter."

When Rosen learned that the creek was considered the headwaters for the famed Everglades, his curiosity—and concern—was ignited. Becoming the driving force behind the idea of highlighting this little-known yet extremely important little stream, he was instrumental in enlisting several sponsors, from government agencies to outfitters. As a result, the expedition quickly took shape, and he helped to organize a send-off at his grand Rosen Shingle Creek Resort that befit a noble quest to slay a dragon. More than two hundred guests came to wish us well on our journey. A helicopter hovered overhead from a local television station. There were numerous dignitaries, media representatives, and a school group bearing gifts. Some of the gifts were humorous—I was given a roll of toilet paper.

We embarked from the resort on the narrow Shingle Creek led by Harris Rosen and his paddling partner, Jena Brooks, director of the Office of Greenways and Trails. They joined us for the first four miles. "This is a dream come true," Harris said of the expedition.

A few miles out, we met with students and teachers from Hunter's Creek Middle School on Shingle Creek. They were curious about our adventure and about the Everglades ecosystem, and it felt good to be around their enthusiasm.

Fig. 4. Students, teachers, and media greet the expedition at Hunter's Creek Middle School along Shingle Creek on the first day.

Besides meeting with students and teachers, we also sought to educate the public through the media. We would highlight various aspects of the region's ecology, from ambitious restoration efforts of the Kissimmee River to unintended threats. For example, chemicals placed on lawns and golf courses in Orlando and other towns along the route could end up in the Everglades system through runoff. Agricultural runoff, mostly from cattle operations, was another concern, along with the introduction of non-native plants and animals that either choked waterways or competed with native wildlife. Like most aquatic systems in Florida, the Upper Everglades had its challenges.

The Hunter's Creek Middle School marked the spot where we were shuttled around two impassable spots in the creek. The waterway fans out into a shallow, snag-filled swamp that might only be navigable in high water. Shingle Creek wasn't always that way. In 1881, Hamilton Disston, son of a wealthy Philadelphia industrialist, purchased 4 million acres of Everglades "swampland" for twenty-five cents an acre and brought steam-powered dredge boats into the northern Everglades. He cut deeper and straighter channels through the Kissimmee River and between the Kissimmee chain of lakes, and created a navigable channel from Lake Okeechobee to the Gulf of Mexico, opening up central Florida to steamboats. Subsequently, a shipping industry began to flourish. Boats docking at the town of Kissimmee were loaded with cypress lumber, sugarcane, pineapples, furs, and other goods. Tourists, immigrant laborers, boatbuilders, and merchants and tradesmen of all sorts flocked to the area.

Eventually, Shingle Creek was dredged and straightened as well. The old spoil berms, covered with cypress and pine, are still visible, mostly along the western shore. The creek itself received its name from early pioneers who used its old-growth cypress trees to make shingles. The settlement of Shingle Creek had a cypress mill and the area's first post office.

Even after the boom started, the environs of Shingle Creek and nearby Kissimmee was a semi-wilderness, and encounters with wild animals were frequent. Elizabeth Cantrell, in *When Kissimmee Was Young*, writes about her father's encounter with a panther in Kissimmee. He was walking a schoolteacher home one night when they met "the savage animal."

He says the scream of the panther is like the voice of a woman terrified beyond all imagination, and is enough to curdle the blood of any one who hears it, and his was no exception. The animal advanced steadily toward them through the swamp as they could tell by the screams and they met at the edge of the cleared space which they were forced to cross. The animal faced them for what seemed minutes, still emitting those frightful screams. As he was armed only with a knife and knew it was madness to turn his back on it, he faced it in desperation, and then by the mercy of Providence, and he can think it nothing less, the great cat slowly turned, and still screaming vanished in the darkness of the swamp.

In *Old Tales and Trails of Florida*, Myrtle Hilliard Crow uses several local sources to describe the area's pioneer life. E.L.D. Overstreet of Shingle Creek, born in 1852, settled in the area in 1856. He creates a vivid picture of life on the Florida frontier: "The woods were filled with bear to eat the hogs, wolves to eat the calves, and panthers to eat the deer. The wild animals came up into the yard. The hogs came to the house at night for protection from the bears. . . . The country was full of Indians who came to the house to sell their goods." Mr. Overstreet pointed out that most settlers were squatters who wandered about until they found a good place to settle. For many years, they feared gangs of Civil War deserters who roamed the countryside.

The major mode of transportation was by various types of boats. "Every settler had his skiff boat or launch and the red-skinned Seminoles used dugout canoes," writes Florida Cracker historian Lawrence E. Will. "We even had store boats and a church boat, too. There were no roads and blamed few trails, so if you didn't have a boat, you just plain stayed at home."

Paul Yates of Kissimmee was raised on the banks of Shingle Creek in the late 1800s. There were the remains of scattered wigwams on the lakeshore, he remembered, and "Kissimmee was a very beautiful place in its original state."

Since the Kissimmee area was sparsely settled in the pioneer days, family deaths were infrequent. According to Nettie Bass Hatch of Kissimmee, a deceased person was usually kept in the house for twenty-four hours. Sometimes boards had to be pried off of the family cabin in order to build a coffin. After burial, the funeral service was often delayed until a traveling preacher made one of his regular circuits through the area.

Game was plentiful in pioneer Florida, and there were no laws regarding hunting. If you had a gun and shells, there was no reason to go hungry. Early accounts were the stuff of legend. One 1880s hunter, Benjamin F. Cobb, claimed that the turkeys were so plentiful that they only picked out the ones with the reddest heads. "One day a man named Crews killed eight while he was cooking grits for breakfast," he said. "The deer were so plentiful that the man walked along and struck the palmettos with a stick and shot them as they started to run away."

Animal skins were a major trade or sale item. One old-timer remembered seeing "a stack of coon skins four feet wide, four feet high, and eight feet long, in the storehouse of Waters and Carson Grocery Company, which was Kissimmee's leading store for many years."

Red wolves were a real problem, according to Aaron Bass of St. Cloud. Cows were penned at night and the calves were allowed to run loose, but "when the wolves got after the calves, the cows stampeded and broke out of the pens, running to their assistance, and fought with their horns and hoofs. Wolves even tried to rob the camps at night, and the only way to get rid of them was to feed them strychnine in the beef. These animals were intelligent enough to know to follow the herds of cattle which were driven through the country and attack the weak or straggling calves that dropped by the wayside."

Eventually, the state government assisted in the eradication of Florida's wolves by offering bounties for pelts. By the 1930s, red wolves were extinct east of the Mississippi. Today, owing to a reintroduction effort, red wolf pups are trained on St. Vincent's Island in north Florida and eventually released in North Carolina at either the Great Smoky Mountains National Park or the Alligator River National Wildlife Refuge.

Freshwater fish from the Kissimmee chain of lakes and tributary streams was another major food source for early pioneers. Laws regarding their harvest were nonexistent. People shot bass with shotguns, speared fish by torchlight, and used nets. According to Mr. and

Mrs. Lee Lanier of Shingle Creek, fishermen used seines up to nine hundred yards in length. They filled barrels with catfish and perch and hauled them by boat to the Makinson Hardware Store in Kissimmee. The fish were then prepared for shipment to northern markets.

Bird life was abundant as well, and even though pioneers killed many kinds of birds for food and feathers, they were also admired. Hannigan Patrick of Orlando, born in 1861, remembered the great flocks: "There were all kinds of beautiful birds, and the woods were alive with animals. Thousands of parakeets also lived in the area and fed on a large field of cockleburs." He was referring to the colorful red, green, and yellow Carolina parakeet, the only parrot native to the eastern United States. Once common, the last wild Carolina parakeet was believed to have been killed in Okeechobee County in 1904, although unverified sightings were reported through the 1920s. The last zoo specimen died in Cincinnati, Ohio, in 1918.

Although some farmers believed that the parakeets helped to control invasive cockleburs in their fields, most farmers viewed them as pests and contributed to their extinction through shooting and poisoning. The birds were also killed for their colorful feathers, which were used as adornments for ladies' hats. Habitat loss was another factor. Some scientists theorize that the birds succumbed to poultry disease. Whatever the reason, the loss of the Carolina parakeet removed a once abundant and colorful bird from the Florida landscape.

Fortunately, the mid-twentieth century marked the advent of conservation laws that prevented several other species from slipping into the abyss of extinction—the Florida panther, Florida black bear, wood stork, American bald eagle, snail kite, and several others. Attempts were made to manage fish and game populations in a sustainable manner. Gone are the days of wanton shooting of birds and animals to the point where guns became too hot to handle, and large-scale seine fishing in freshwater has been outlawed throughout the state except in Lake Okeechobee during normal water levels. Today, Shingle Creek and the Kissimmee chain of lakes are often enjoyed for their natural beauty as much as for the fish and game that the land and waters produce.

The night before we embarked on the expedition, I called my friend Ed Winn of Maitland. In his seventies, Winn was born and raised in

Fig. 5. Film crew on Shingle Creek during the first day of the expedition. Photo by Bob Mindick.

the Orlando area, and he often writes about Florida history and volunteers as a storyteller in the schools. "Shingle Creek!" he exclaimed when I told him of our starting point. "Why, that's where I used to catch water moccasins just for the fun of it. Found nineteen or twenty the last time I was there."

It's just the kind of thing you want to hear right before a trip, reminding me of a time when two friends and I were traveling to the Glacier Park area in Montana to help build a log cabin. When we stopped at the last town before our destination, one old-timer warned us about grizzly bears. "You're just one big ham to them," he said to the wide-eyed Floridians.

On Shingle Creek, I only spotted one small black snake wriggling through the water, but I carefully scanned the shore each time I stepped out of my kayak.

So where does the water run from this headwater stream, a place where cypress shingles were once made and water moccasins were caught for fun? It flows south ever slowly through "that fine chain of lakes which scatter up and down the center of Florida, like bright beads from a string," as Marjory Stoneman Douglas describes in *The Everglades: River of Grass*.

The lakes are part of the Kissimmee valley, a wide, shallow sag formed over time by percolating water and underground aquifers that dissolved the limestone base. From the last lake in the chain, Lake Kissimmee, the water runs through both the channelized and restored sections of the Kissimmee River before spilling into Lake Okeechobee, Florida's largest body of freshwater. The entire Kissimmee valley south of Orlando drains a massive 2,500 square miles. Lacking any deep chasms, the water flows down a "valley" slope that drops only two inches per mile.

Canals have replaced sheet flow through the massive agricultural area south of Lake Okeechobee, but then the water fans out through what is still an impressive "river of grass." This is the image that most people conjure up when they think of the Everglades—a vast, windswept expanse where grass and water act as natural canvases for the paintbrushes of sun and clouds.

And then the water flows through a myriad of mangrove-lined streams into Florida Bay and mixes with salty waters of the Gulf of Mexico and Atlantic Ocean, even ending up at the Keys' famous coral reefs. The water may not be permanently separated from Shingle Creek, however. Evaporation through the entire system, and from the seas, may form rain clouds that return the water to its source, feeding Shingle Creek through a number of smaller streams and canals. As Douglas pointed out, the Everglades does not depend upon melting snow or large cavernous springs—"Here the rain is everything."

chapter 2

~~~~~~~~~~~~~~~~~~~~~

Lake Toho's Incredible Island

A strong headwind blasted us by the time we had followed Shingle Creek to its terminus at Lake Tohopekaliga on that first day. At nearly 19,000 acres, what is commonly referred to as "Lake Toho" had an oceanlike feel. We struggled against wind and choppy waves to reach the 132-acre Makinson Island, one of many large islands that dot the Kissimmee chain of lakes. We landed on a sandy beach area near a dock and pitched tents in a grassy meadow behind old-growth live oaks that ringed much of the island. The sun shone brightly, warming the air enough for us to be comfortable in short pants; the constant breeze kept mosquitoes at bay. What more could we ask for?

We quickly discovered that Makinson Island, once slated to become a resort hotel and time-share development and now publicly owned, was a place with nesting bald eagles, swooping snail kites, and numerous wading birds and sandhill cranes. This was once home to Seminole Indians. Some suggest the Seminole name for the island was the same as the lake—Tohopekaliga, or "fort site." During the Second Seminole War, thick trees provided the Seminoles with cover, and canoes were kept on opposite ends of the island so that escape from soldiers was always possible. Seminole leaders Coacoochee, or Wildcat, and his father, King Philip, are said to have frequented the island. Some have claimed that Coacoochee was born on the island, but different sources point to different locations. At this point, I'm not sure anyone knows for sure.

Fig. 6. Dale Allen paddling into Lake Toho.

After the Seminoles were driven from the area, the island was known by many names, such as Olive, Cypress, and Dickerman, depending upon the owner and era. After the state purchased the island in 1999, it was officially given the name most used by longtime area residents, Makinson Island, after pioneer entrepreneur W. B. Makinson Sr. The store he founded, Makinson Hardware, is the longest operational business in the town of Kissimmee, opened the year after the town was founded in 1883.

Beth and I hiked around the island, scaring up exotic sheep and spotting bald eagles. While the island's interior is mostly improved pasture, its fringe is generally unspoiled. We walked the shoreline beneath a canopy of sabal palms, cypress trees, and the arching limbs of live oaks. It was easy to visualize Seminole warriors perched atop the trees, scanning the lake for approaching soldiers.

According to pioneer accounts of the Second Seminole War in the Kissimmee area, months of relative quiet would be followed by sudden violence. White people would be killed and homesteads burned by warring Seminoles. Some settlers claimed they were alerted to the

Fig. 7. Old-growth live oaks, festooned with beards of Spanish moss, bordered the Makinson Island camp on the first night of expedition.

presence of Seminoles by their cattle—when they scented the Seminoles in the air, they would sometimes stampede. Worried settlers would flee to Fort Gatlin or other nearby forts, but, since food was often in short supply, the men would eventually venture out again to hunt and plant or harvest crops.

Lake Toho's islands were considered fertile ground for growing crops because of the ebb and flow of lake waters that left behind rich sediments. So it wasn't surprising that Isaac Jernigan began paddling a dugout canoe to Jernigan Island during the Second Seminole War in order to plant crops. The island is adjacent to Makinson Island and is now called Paradise Island, also publicly owned. To his dismay, Jernigan glanced back and spotted a Seminole warrior paddling a dugout in hot pursuit. Not wanting to be trapped in the confines of an island, Jernigan landed in present-day Kissimmee and ran to a swamp that lay just west of the current business district. The warrior followed.

Jernigan's shoes, being soaked, made so much noise that he cut the strings and left them. He climbed a tree and hid behind thick, moss-draped branches until his pursuer gave up. He then walked barefoot to Fort Gatlin, bruised and cut by the underbrush.

After the war, the Seminoles who had not been killed or removed to Oklahoma hid in the Everglades, eventually returning to the Kissimmee area. Relations were generally friendly between whites and Indians, with some exceptions. In Myrtle Hilliard Crow's *Old Tales and Trails of Florida*, John L. Bronson of Kissimmee recollected: "Tom Tiger Tail was building a canoe when he was struck by lightning. He was placed in his canoe and enclosed with the usual pen. Some people from Washington removed the remains to that city. The Indians were very angry, and their threat of 'Kill white people heap ojus' alarmed the whites. Word was sent to Washington, and the remains were returned to their last resting-place." Tiger Tail's remains were of interest to the Smithsonian because of his large stature.

Fig. 8. A bald eagle perched atop a dead snag on Makinson Island in Lake Tohopekaliga.

Cultural differences were stark between the two cultures, and some were humorous. Mamie White-Thomas of Hilliard's Island in East Lake Toho recalled the day when, as a child, two Seminoles came to her house. Her mother urged her to go see them, but the child didn't think the Indians were properly dressed. "I don't want to go in there," she said. "They are in their shirt tails." At the time, Seminole men commonly wore long shirts but no pants in the warm climate.

Appropriately, for our first expedition dinner, Julia organized a pioneer-style barbecue of wild hog and other Cracker fare and brought along members of the Osceola County Historical Society. The gray-haired historians instructed anyone who was interested in the art of cracking a cow whip. The term "Florida Crackers" is sometimes reported to be derived from the practice of this art by early Florida "cow hunters" during the era of free-range cattle and by persons driving teams of animals. The term "cowboy" was coined later. If her skill at the whip offered any indication, Julia would have made a good cow hunter.

According to Lamb Savage in a 1953 *Florida Wildlife* article, "King of the Crackers," a Florida Cracker was "a person of distinction, someone to be respected and looked up to, but, mind you, to be feared, too, by his enemies. The Cracker of olden days earned the title the hard way. Believe me, it wasn't given to him unless he deserved it. If a man could drive his team of oxen through the timberlands, crack the whip over the animals' heads without touching ' em, and at the same time communicate in bullwhip code with his buddies on ' tother side of the woods, he was a true Cracker."

Lamb grew up just east of Orlando near Fort Christmas, and as a boy he helped to break a sandy trail through the woods to Orlando. He described a way of life of only three or four generations distant that bears little resemblance to the lifestyles of area residents today:

We lived well, raised our own supplies, including rice, tobacco, sugarcane and cotton. My mother used to spin, card and weave the cotton we raised into cloth which was dyed brown with black jack bark and blue with indigo weed. Father made our shoes from cow hide and sewed them with hog bristles in a homemade steel needle. The lasts were made of hickory wood. Mother was the only doctor in our community. She made her own medicines from herbs and weeds and products of the forest. For chills and fever she made a blue grass candy from a grass with a yellow root. She rolled pills from clear drops of pine gum out of a tree where bugs had worked out and the rosin drops came through in soft balls. These she rolled in flour and gave them with the syrup. Chills and fever disappeared before the ninth day with this medication. She boiled vanilla leaves and made a salve for sores. Her eye salve was made from a fuzzy weed that looked like it had tiny drops of water on it, called the honey dew weed. She had a remedy for every ailment and in most cases it was effective.

Boys in those days learned early to do a man's work. When I wuz 12 I cud crack a bull whip 15 feet long over my team, and by the time I wuz 21 I had the old rawhide sending up smoke signals. We learned to shoot straight and talk straight. If we made a man a promise, it was kept.

Once darkness set in, members of the historical society told stories and shared area history around a crackling fire. One tale was of a 1800s feud between a fugitive cattleman named Moses Barber and the county sheriff, David Mizell. "They never liked each other," said the storyteller Dick Simmons, who was once the city manager of Palm Beach. "When Mizell tried to serve a warrant on him, Moses shot him dead. He executed at least nine more people and got away."

Telling these stories, said one man, would help us "better understand the spirits that might be here." There's something about a fire that makes a perfect setting for such talk. "We want to be able to continue to use property like this," concluded Simmons.

Retiring to my tent, I paused briefly to gaze upon the glow of lights from Disney World. Millions of people annually visit Orlando to escape to fantasy worlds, while our small group had come to experience a Florida of shrinking boundaries—old, enduring, and rich beyond belief.

Falling asleep and staying asleep that night was difficult, and it wasn't due to any spirits that roamed the island. Screech owls, scrounging raccoons, crying limpkins, and croaking pig frogs made their presence known. Nature's sounds do not always produce a peaceful ser-

Fig. 9. A cozy fire illuminates faces as historians share stories and history of the Kissimmee area with expedition members camped on Makinson Island.

enade when the decibel level reaches a certain point. Then, sometime after midnight, the sheep herd that grazes the island's grassy interior decided to roam through our camp, bleating loudly, closely followed by grunting wild pigs. Makinson Island refused to sleep and wanted us to join in its slumber party.

George Henry Preble wrote of a similar experience while camping on the banks of the Kissimmee River in 1842: "The day was rendered harmonious by the warblings of multitudes of feathered choristers, and the night hideous with the splash of alligators, hooting of owls, and the screamings of a variety of unquiet night-birds."

When I did sleep, I dreamed of a large buffalo roaming the island. A buffalo? To many native people, the buffalo represents the earth and life. I took it as a good sign.

At the first light of dawn, we woke to the motorized scream of dozens of tournament bass-fishing boats, racing to their secret spots. Lake Tohopekaliga is a bass-fishing mecca, as evidenced by the numerous tracks cut through the weeds by boat propellers. Songbirds, ducks, sandhill cranes, and numerous wading birds were also awakened. We heard their cries and glimpsed them as they fled the loud boats.

Anchorwoman Virginia Johnson of Bright House Networks later commented in an on-air interview about her first night camping with the group: "Nobody told me that they had wild boars on the island. So we set up camp in the middle of the night. I just hear this scratching and this honk, snort, snort, snort, and I wake up, and I'm like, that's a wild boar, man, but I don't know what to do, and I was too afraid to call for help ' cause I thought it would bring him to me. So, I just lay there and I tried not to breathe for like two hours."

We broke camp; it was time to continue the journey. Once we paddled past the windbreak that the island provided, a strong easterly breeze pushed us along and again gave the lake a choppy, oceanlike feel. This wasn't the first time I had been on Lake Toho, but the circumstances were far different. In 2001, I accompanied the Florida Fish and Wildlife Conservation Commission biologist Marty Mann in an airboat as he showed me how excess nutrients from urban and agricultural runoff had prompted a riot of watery plant growth. "Areas that were fishable and wade-able twenty to thirty years ago are now covered in exotic weeds," he said. "Those areas [of weeds] have very low oxygen levels. Few fish, birds, or other life forms can be found there."

One of the main culprits smothering Lake Toho was hydrilla, originally brought into the United States from Ceylon, now Sri Lanka, in the early 1950s for the aquarium trade. A Tampa tropical fish and plant farmer obtained some of the plants from a St. Louis dealer who had thought they were another species of anacharis, which was commonly sold in aquarium stores. The Tampa dealer didn't like the color or overall appearance, but instead of throwing the plants away, he told his manager to do whatever he liked with them. The manager stored them in a wire cage in a canal directly behind their business and forgot about them. Months later, he was surprised that the plant had spread throughout the canal. The dealer recognized a golden opportunity and started marketing the prolific plant as "Indian starvine."

Quantities purchased by a Miami business were allowed to escape to a nearby creek. After that, hydrilla clinging to boat propellers or dumped out of aquariums helped to spread the infestation. The plant was mistaken for a native species for several years, but in 1965, the scientists Lyle Weldon and Bob Blackburn noticed that "Indian starvine" had a subterranean tuber attached to its roots, unlike the similar-looking native species. They correctly named the plant *Hydrilla verticillata*, but by then, the invasive plant was in Florida to stay, to be kept in check primarily by periodic applications of herbicide. Sadly, in 1972, Weldon became entangled in hydrilla while scuba diving and lost his life.

To remedy Lake Toho's problems in 2001, the commission planned a water drawdown since water levels can be artificially managed by locks throughout the system below the lake. Bulldozers would then remove 4 million cubic yards of muck and miles of exotic aquatic plants that have smothered fish spawning grounds. The lake's original sandy bottom would be visible for the first time in years. "It's the only way the lake will survive," Marty Mann said. "Afterward, it will be a matter of maintaining it and weeding it like a garden."

Mann proved to be right. The drawdown was successful; fish and bird populations benefited and the lake opened up. What remains to be seen is whether future drawdowns will be necessary since people and cows still live along Lake Toho and its tributaries, feeding the system with excess nutrients. Lakes throughout the entire system also underwent drawdowns for the same reasons.

The ability to do drawdowns in Lake Toho hinged on the public purchase of Makinson Island in 1999. If the previous landowners, developers Richard Dickerman and then Gary Hock, had succeeded in subdividing the island into five-acre lots and auctioning them, twenty-five wealthy landowners would likely have opposed drawdowns since they would have been unable to reach their homes or the mainland by boat. The Trust for Public Land (TPL), acting as "undevelopers," served as intermediaries for the state, negotiating the purchases of both Makinson Island and the nearby Paradise Island. They had to move quickly. "Hock had a lot of people lined up to buy the land, and we just stepped in at the right time and put our money where our mouth is," said Bob Guido, southeast projects manager for TPL. Jeb Bush, governor at the time, was critical of the $4 million purchase price, but Guido defended the cost since public ownership of the islands was critical for the lake drawdowns. "As far as economics go, the lake is 18,810 acres," he told me afterward, "and when you look at 18,810 acres of lake, the preservation of these islands contributed to the overall preservation of the entire lake."

My weed-choked lake tour with Marty Mann was my first time in an airboat. Powered by an airplane engine—noisy beyond belief—the skimming craft was about the only way to move across thick mats of hyacinth and hydrilla. It is the preferred means of travel for many who move through the Everglades system. Still, the poor birds. Shooting across weeds and marsh, I felt pity for the ducks as they frantically flapped their wings to escape the whirling monster. I know a bird-watcher friend who, at age twelve, saw her first purple gallinule on an Everglades airboat tour. The boat ran it over. "Don't worry, little lady," the driver shouted over her screams, "they pop back up!"

In 2006, I was given the opportunity to drive an airboat along the Gulf by a public lands manager. After giving some initial instruction with the stick that served as a steering wheel, owing to the noise my teacher had to scream any additional directions. "Don't stop too fast," he yelled, "or the backwash will fill the rear of the boat, and this thing will sink like a rock."

On smooth water, an airboat feels like a noisy magic carpet, hovering ethereally just above the water's surface. The sensation helps one to understand the attraction to the beasts. On the other hand, in choppy conditions, an airboat is a jarring, seasick-inducing vehicle, not seaworthy in the least. And by being perched up high and fully exposed, you feel like you're moving through a blizzard if the air is the least bit cold. On one bumpy, cold ride, the screws in my sunglass handles jarred loose, and for a half hour afterward, my freezing nose rivaled Rudolph's. Give me a kayak any day.

As we bobbed up and down while paddling across Lake Toho, Bob pointed to an unspoiled cypress-lined shoreline to the north. "We [Osceola County] own all of that land," he said. "We're going to develop it into a park. It will be a great rest stop for future paddlers." Since the park wasn't yet open, we stopped for a rest break at a "members and guests only" resort development just past the public land. Bob humorously planted his orange caution flag in the soft soil alongside the landing in a gesture reminiscent of early European explorers claiming New World territory. We used the restroom, ordered juice at the resort's bar, and were warmly welcomed, even though we weren't

Fig. 10. Sandhill cranes were a common sight on the expedition. Photo by Bob Mindick.

members or invited guests. Local news coverage of our expedition had helped to open doors with strangers.

We moved along the lake's western shore behind a line of marsh grass since the east wind was now hitting us broadside. Bob stopped to explain to the documentary crew about exotic plants and critters that had made their way into the Kissimmee chain of lakes. Standing on one of the muck piles created by the scraping of the lake bottom, he pointed to prickly tropical soda apple plants around his feet. "These originally came from South America, and now the seeds are spread through cow dung," he said.

Another worrisome exotic is the island apple snail, first imported by the aquarium trade from South America. This whorled snail is similar in appearance to the native apple snail, but it grows larger, has deeper grooves or channels on its shell, and multiplies in greater numbers. While native apple snail populations are declining, its exotic cousin is on the rise. Two increasingly rare native birds depend on the apple snail for survival—the limpkin and snail kite. Limpkins have been observed eating exotic snails in Everglades National Park, but snail kites have not. The exotic snails are also voracious feeders on aquatic vegetation, including desirable native species such as eelgrass. They are believed to harbor parasites that could be dangerous to humans if consumed, so escargot was not on our menu for the evening.

Earlier, Bob had showed us the difference between native apple snail eggs and island apple snail eggs. Both lay clusters of eggs out of the water on tree trunks, cypress knees, and emergent vegetation, but the exotic snail eggs are bright pink and usually in clusters of several hundred, while the native snail eggs are whiter and in clusters of ten to eighty eggs. One control method is to simply scrape the exotic eggs into the water since the eggs must be dry to hatch.

Our destination was the Southport Fish Camp, and soon after we landed by the boat ramp, a bystander asked, "How far are you going in those rowboats?" It was obvious that people weren't used to seeing kayaks in the chain of lakes.

The fish camp owner was gracious and offered us a free "monster wildlife tour." Our means of transport was the land version of an airboat—a gargantuan swamp buggy. The tires alone were six feet in diameter. Just to reach the beast from the ground, we had to climb a

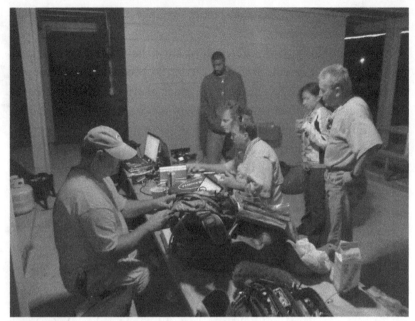

Fig. 11. Every evening, the film crew worked on their daily television news clips while expedition members wrote a blog.

long ramp. Once under way, we entered an 8,000-acre private ranch across the street where we were trucked through scenic live oak hammocks and treated to sightings of deer, turkey, sandhill crane, raccoon, Sherman's fox squirrel, red-shouldered hawk, and armadillo.

That evening, Julia organized another traditional Osceola County feast. The aromas of fried frog legs, alligator tail, and catfish filled our camp. Side dishes included roast corn, strings beans, coleslaw, and an exotic delight—bananas flambeau. Bananas were split in the peel, inserted with chocolate, and coated with rum. Then, the creation was lit with a long lighter and voila! Bananas flambeau! It was a great way to celebrate the successful conclusion of the expedition's second day.

chapter 3

Passageways

Four bald eagles greeted us as we exited Southport—three adults and one juvenile. They hovered, circled, and one posed for us on a cypress tree limb. Many times I have heard native people express their reverence for birds, especially eagles.

"The eagle flies highest in the sky of all the birds and so he is the nearest to the Creator, and his feather is the most sacred of all," said Seminole elder Buffalo Jim in the book *Wisdomkeepers*. "He is the highest of the birds and so belongs to all tribes, to all the peoples."

We entered C-35, the first of several locks we would encounter on the trip. It took about fifteen minutes for us to be lowered about four feet so we could exit out into the C-35 or Southport Canal. The locks were built for flood control in response to hurricanes in the 1940s and 1950s that flooded towns such as Kissimmee for several weeks. They also serve to offset the fast-draining effects of canals by maintaining the upper lakes at a higher water level.

The Southport Canal, one of many dredged in the 1880s, had an immediate effect of lowering lake levels in Lake Toho. Archie Williams observed the changes in 1882, noting that orange groves were being planted in former floodplains, and land originally purchased "for a trifle" was selling for more than $100 an acre. Several islands that were previously inundated during high-water periods were no longer being flooded, adding to their value.

Figs. 12, 13. The Kissimmee chain of lakes has one of the highest concentrations of nonmigratory bald eagles in the continental United States.

Standing upon recently drained land along the unfinished South-port Canal, Williams concluded:

Eight months ago, the ground upon which we stand was covered by surface water to a depth of from one to two feet; today it stands, high and dry, two feet above the level of the lake and the canal, the great instrument of the reclamation not yet cut through. As we walk across the land, we crush beneath our feet the dried and dead water lilies, cresses and lettuce, which a few months ago grew, bloomed and flourished in their natural element (the water), and in their place the familiar switch cane of Louisiana, the sure indication of rich alluvial land, is fast taking possession of the soil. It, too, may grow and flourish for a few months longer, but as Louisiana's hand directed the great work which wrested and reclaimed this, the richest land in the South, from the water, so will a Louisianian's hand perfect what has already been done, by showing how sugar cane can be made to grow and yield by Louisiana cultivation upon Florida soil.

Fig. 14. Expedition member Bob Mindick pulls the horn to alert the lock tender to open the gates at one of several locks that regulate water levels in the system.

Not surprisingly, Williams was promoting the positive effects of dredging and drainage as part of an expedition sponsored by Louisiana's *New Orleans Times-Democrat*. His words proved to be prophetic. One of the first crops to be successfully grown on the newly drained land was sugarcane; the first tract was planted in February 1884. The initial yields per acre set records, largely due to natural fertilizers in the lake sediments. Florida's "Big Sugar" industry was born. A sugar mill was built in St. Cloud, and sugar became an export product until the industry disappeared after the turn of the twentieth century with the lifting of federal subsidies and the cane borers that were inadvertently introduced from Cuba.

Today, land bordering the Southport Canal appears pastoral and is primarily used for cattle grazing. Occasional live oak trees provide welcome shade, live oaks that had grown up since the dredging more than a century before. The scenes were reminiscent of the more "civilized" countryside of Europe.

Still, for the kayaker, it was a bit boring. "Monotonous," was how Dale described it. "No shade, less wildlife by far," he said. Unlike a winding, tree-canopied stream, a straight canal takes away the mystery of wondering what is around the bend; you can see a mile or more downstream.

The Southport Canal accounted for 3.5 miles of the more than 40 miles of canal dug through the Upper Everglades system by 1885, according to James M. Kreamer, chief engineer and general superintendent for Hamilton Disston's drainage company. The construction resulted in more than 1 million acres of "permanently drained" land, according to Kreamer. Although that figure was disputed, the company optimistically reported that their next goal was the drainage of 7 million acres, or almost the entire Everglades.

Disston's untimely death in 1886 at age fifty-two, followed by the financial crisis of 1893, caused the demise of Disston's company. His dream lived on, however. Other drainage projects continued through the next century, reducing the size of the Everglades by more than half.

The original waterway connecting Lake Toho and Cypress Lake and the winding waterways connecting other lakes in the chain were all referred to as the Kissimmee River by early travelers. The astute Williams in 1882 made another announcement that proved prophetic regarding the old Kissimmee River channel:

> The river, previous to the dredging of the canal, was navigable, so far as depth of water was concerned, for small steamers about 4 feet, but since the canal has lowered the waters of the lake the river is hardly navigable for small boats, and ere many months go by, the Kissimmee river, between Lakes Cypress and Tohopotaliga [sic], will be a thing of the past, leaving naught behind to remind one of the past existence except the line of willows and oaks, which fringe its banks, and a dry bed of white sand which once was its bottom.

When we climbed the banks of the canal and looked to the west, we saw a line of trees in the distance. Was this the old channel? The map didn't show anything clearly.

After more than three miles of canal paddling, we approached Cypress Lake and were thrilled to see a roseate spoonbill feeding in the marsh—a colorful sentry for this natural lake. In the early 1880s, a Jacksonville taxidermist paid five dollars apiece for "pink curleys"—a tempting amount of money in those days. A few years later, a pair of spoonbill wings could fetch seven dollars a pair, enough money to feed a frontier family for several days or more. In New York City, just an ounce of the pink feathers brought twenty dollars. As a result, spoonbills were nearly decimated, their wings used for fans and their feathers for hat adornments. By 1939, only fifteen breeding pairs were believed to remain in Florida. Owing to aggressive conservation measures, numbers have risen since that time to maybe a thousand breeding pairs.

Once we were on Cypress Lake, the undulating lake shoreline was a welcome relief from the alleyway of the canal. We hugged the shallows along the undeveloped north shore to buffer a stiff headwind, weaving in and out of stands of bulrushes. Flocks of moorhens, red-winged blackbirds, and white pelicans added color and melody. With the exception of occasional mats of exotic hydrilla, it was easy to imagine the lake as it had been centuries before.

Airboats lined the shore in front of the Cypress Lake RV and Fishing Resort, our destination. These Old Florida fish camps are becom-

Fig. 15. Roseate spoonbills are one of the striking birds seen along the Kissimmee valley. The birds were once hunted extensively for their pink feathers. Photo by Bob Mindick.

ing rare in other parts of Florida but are still common along the Kissimmee chain of lakes.

After setting up camp, Dale starting poring over maps and asking questions of Vince Matera and Ayounga Riddick with the water management district. He was looking for an alternative to paddling the canal between Cypress Lake and Lake Hatchineha. "Is this the original channel?" he asked, pointing to a winding stream called the Dead River.

"That's it," said Vince. "At first it runs through a pasture, and it might have some low spots, but once it meets up with Reedy Creek, it's real nice and natural looking. On another trip, you should really paddle up Reedy Creek to Lake Russell. Now that is wild and beautiful."

Bill Graf, the media liaison for the district, added that Reedy Creek, which drains Disney World, is very clean. "Disney planned a state-of-the-art drainage system well in advance of development," he said, "unlike most of Orlando."

Ayounga was nervous because the motorboat that carried the documentary crew—and offered a safety net in case there was trouble or we became lost—wouldn't be able to make it up the shallow creek. "We should stick to the plan," he said, referring to paddling the canal. Ayounga, a district land manager for most of the chain of lakes, had been extremely helpful in numerous ways, especially in providing us with key GPS points of major junctions, but he hadn't included the Dead River in his calculations. Since we had no chain of command on the trip, however—meaning that there was no central leader—the majority won out.

"You have to be careful in there," Vince cautioned. "It's not a state park."

I wondered how the Dead River received its name—had much of its lifeblood been drained after the canal was built? No one knew.

After a night of sleep interrupted by a cow that wandered through the campground bellowing loudly—a pitiful sound that seemed to say, "I'm lost!"—Beth, Mike, and Dale and I began paddling across the lake toward the Dead River, boosted by a stiff tailwind. Bob decided to follow the itinerary and take the canal. He preferred using the bicycle apparatus on his kayak as an alternative to paddling, and it didn't work in shallow water. Ian decided to keep him company.

The first challenge was in finding the Dead River. We missed the opening and paddled along the lake's edge an extra mile. A kind FWC officer in an airboat directed us to the correct spot—a near-invisible weed-choked channel through the marsh. "You be careful in there," he said. "You could easily turn the wrong way and end up in the middle of a swamp and then not know which way is which. A lot of blind curves. There have been people killed in airboat accidents in there."

A good send-off.

I didn't realize until months later, while scanning newspaper clippings of the area, that one of those killed on the Dead River was a

Fig. 16. Cypress knees along the Dead River.

friend of mine, Richard Coleman. He was driving an airboat in 2003 and had a head-on collision with another airboat; the other driver was charged with reckless driving. A founding member of the Florida chapter of the Sierra Club, Coleman was a champion of Kissimmee River restoration and was one of the most effective activists I had ever been around. He gained the trust and respect of hunters, anglers, airboaters, and environmentalists because he shared all of their interests. A camping area where we would stay on the southern end of Lake Kissimmee would later be named the Coleman Landing Shady Oaks Recreation Area in honor of Richard.

Once on the Dead River, the channel did seem a bit lifeless—coursing through a barren-looking cattle ranch. Cows moved along in bunches and sometimes jumped out of the river as we approached. Even though the water management district now owned this land, a cattle lease runs through 2020, and it would likely be renewed. Clumps of cypress trees seemed out of place on high ground. We had to step out of our kayaks on several occasions and drag the boats through shallow sections.

At one spot, two wild-looking horses stood in the narrow channel munching water weeds. They didn't seem the least bit disturbed by us, but soon a huge airboat carrying sightseers pulled behind me, sightseers who had paid forty-five dollars each. I hugged the bank as it passed while tourists snapped photos of the unusual kayakers, but then the boat stopped for the horses to move. I was caught behind the propeller, forced to endure wind, waves, and incredible noise. Somehow this was not the idyllic paddle we had envisioned.

When we merged with Reedy Creek, we stopped for lunch, and the airboat stopped there, too. We exchanged greetings with the operator. He nodded to Beth's kayak and smiled, "You gotta be careful with that blue canoe," he said. "It's gator mating season, and they'll think that's a female gator!"

Fig. 17. Free-range horses curiously eye a kayaker as they graze along the Dead River near Lake Cypress.

Fig. 18. An airboat approaches a kayak in the narrow Dead River.

After the Reedy Creek junction, the channel was more winding and natural looking, with lush aromatic willow trees and cypress bases that actually touched the water. Briefly, I had the illusion that we were the first to paddle this natural passageway between lakes, but I knew better. Over millennia, countless native people had paddled the same creek in their dugouts, overlapped by Europeans in the past few hundred years.

Perhaps the earliest recorded expedition through the region occurred in the spring of 1842. Guided by the Seminole Indian John Tiger Tail and his wife, Fanny, Rear Admiral George Henry Preble and a detachment of fifty-one sailors and twenty-four marines paddled sixteen, thirty-foot dugouts up the Kissimmee River and through the chain of lakes. For two months they searched in vain for Seminoles who had escaped removal. Along the way, they feasted on cranes, crane eggs, crane livers, rattlesnake, raccoon, deer, turtles, alligator tails, water turkeys, and curlew (ibis). More than once, "foolish fish" jumped into their canoes and quickly ended up in the frying pan.

Disappointed at not killing or capturing any Seminoles, only find-ing signs of their camps, they made a habit of digging up Seminole graves. Preble penned this account on March 15, 1842:

Cool and cloudy, wind N.E.; at 9 A.M. landed and examined a live-oak hummock where Indians had been dressing deerskins not more than two weeks back. At 9:30 landed at another hum-mock where was a large mound out of which Fanny, the Indian wife of our Guide, assured us she had seen money, breastplates, and beads dug. Set the men to work with their paddles, promis-ing them good current money for all they found in the mound; excavated quite a trench, but found nothing but a few bones and blue glass beads.

In one lake, a lieutenant and twenty-four men explored an island and "returned with an Indian's knife and skull which he had found in a grave."

Natural passageways from what is likely Lake Hatchineha to Lake Tohopekaliga were described in this account from March 20th:

Started at 6 A.M. through the grass in search of Benham's stream [Benham was a member of their party who had scouted the stream the day before]; entered, pulled a few miles, crossed an-other small lake [Cypress Lake?], and entered the stream once more from its N.E. extremity. The stream winding, narrow, and rapid. Dined under a moss-drooping cypress. Afternoon: Stream winding through tangled bushes, interlaced from either bank; outlet of Lake Tohopeteliga [sic]; found there fresh moccasin tracks and roots newly dug, the ground still freshly turned as if hastily abandoned; pieces of orange-peel were strewed about.

Fortunately, no one in our contemporary expedition party endured the hardships of Fanny. March 29, 1842: "Fanny went into the woods and gave birth to a still-born infant; buried it herself and returned to camp, and resumed her usual duties."

By journey's end, Preble himself suffered from badly inflamed and ulcerated feet and legs—"poisoned by the saw-grass of the Everglades and exposure to the mud, through which we dragged our canoes, and the effects of the sun." After the journey, doctors threatened to amputate both limbs. Preble kept his legs, but "it was more than two years before all the sores were healed, and for years after I felt the effects of these sixty days in a dug-out canoe in Florida."

Nearing the end of the Dead River, we concluded that this alternate route would be enjoyed by paddlers, especially if the water were higher, and that it should be an option in any future paddling guide. I took several GPS points.

In the future, original connector channels such as the Dead River will likely be benefited by efforts to undo past wrongs. The South Florida Water Management District has purchased vast tracts of former floodplain along the entire watershed—more than 100,000 acres in all at an average cost of $3,000 per acre—so the chain of lakes and Kissimmee River can once again pulse with the ebb and flow of wet and dry seasons, thus enhancing the health of wetlands and fish and wildlife populations. The state of Florida and local governments have been buying additional tracts for recreation and wildlife protection.

However, complete restoration of the chain of lakes basin is not possible unless entire communities are moved, so canals connecting the lakes and associated locks and dams will remain to maintain enough water for boat traffic and to prevent severe flooding of nearby towns and cities, such as Kissimmee. The locks will be used to create a controlled degree of flooding that will prevent property damage and yet mimic natural cycles that are essential to the ecology of the lakes, wetlands, and the restored section of the Kissimmee River below the lakes. The district bought enough land to allow flooding up to fifty-four feet above sea level, more than a foot higher than the previous level. Historically, the chain of lakes may have flooded at fifty-five feet or higher, high enough to inundate present-day towns for several weeks.

The purchases also ensure that the shores along the chain of lakes, especially below Lake Toho, will largely remain undeveloped. Dale, who is in the business of buying lands for parks for the Trust for Public Land, seemed more impressed with each passing day by the abundant wildlife and aesthetic beauty. "This trip has been an eye-opener for me," he said. "I had no idea there was so much natural beauty and protected land in this part of rapidly developing Florida."

For private landowners, however, selling land for conservation and public uses can be bittersweet. In 2001, I visited a 2,350-acre tract along Lake Istokpoga, which feeds into the Kissimmee River via the Istokpoga canal, for *Florida Wildlife* magazine. Known then as the Silver Harbor Ranch, and now as the Royce Unit of the Lake Wales Ridge Wildlife and Environmental Area, it was the first candidate for purchase under a new state acquisition program that dawned with the twenty-first century—Florida Forever. Since then, Florida Forever, funded by the state at a rate of $300 million a year, has purchased more than a half million acres of natural Florida. Acquisition of the Silver Harbor Ranch fit in with efforts to protect the northern Everglades system. The problem was that the deal was not yet sealed when I visited, so I was in for a surprise.

Upon my arrival, I was graciously received by Steve Royce and his brother, Ray Jr.; they managed the property. Ray, big-boned and dark-haired, was the older of the two, while Steve was more wiry and fair-haired. With tape recorder in hand, I followed the brothers into their small wooden office and asked some basic questions about the tract.

I quickly learned that Steve and Ray would just as soon their family kept the property. Their feelings were understandable. Home for them was an unmarred expanse of pastures, pine forests, and swamps sweeping down to an unspoiled lakeshore. But Steve and Ray had been outvoted by other family members who preferred to sell the property. Their fledgling hunting and ecotourism business, along with cattle grazing and a small orange grove, wasn't generating big revenues. Land values were skyrocketing, and so were taxes—a common story throughout Florida. Why not sell it to the state for conservation?

Here's how the conversation went:

UNKNOWING JOURNALIST: How long has your family owned the
   property?
RAY: Since the twenties; our great-grandfather bought it. We had
   some real good memories as kids. We'd come over here with
   our grandparents and sit by the fire and cook hamburgers.
   We'd do everything from helping to round up cattle to enjoying the wildlife.

STEVE: In the late seventies, our grandfather, who was kind of managing the property, turned a tractor over and got killed out here. At that point, Ray came from college and started working on it. I came a few years later. . . . About four or five years ago, we got into the outdoor recreation business. We'd put people in the cabin for overnight stays, we did guided quail hunts, and let people shoot sporting clays.

RAY: We've done a lot of what we've envisioned as improvements and pastures and clearings, rotational grazing, chopping, burning. Since the time we've been here, we've seen the favorable change in the number of species that are out here, and the species populations. We've seen the Sherman fox squirrels populations explode. We've seen the turkey populations explode. We're seeing more and more gopher tortoises. Because we've kind of cleaned it out, the numbers of the sandhill cranes are increasing. And we still have areas that have the scrub jays and skinks and all that. It's been interesting for us to see that as we've become better and better property managers, to see those species continue to develop.

STEVE: It takes a lot of work to keep out the exotic plants—the soda apple and the Florida holly (Brazilian pepper). I don't know that the state has the funding, the manpower, or even the desire to manage it as intensely. They're going to want a lot of these improved pastures to go back to native range. That I can understand. Eventually, they're even going to want the orange groves to die out and grow back into the native scrub that was there. I question whether they're really going to be able to keep out some of the exotic plants, keep out the poachers that live along our border, that sort of stuff.

The main exotic is the tropical soda apple. It's very invasive and it will take over quickly if you don't stay after it. I've been down to the Immokalee and LaBelle area, where there's thousands and thousands of acres of it. Florida holly is not as big a problem because it grows so much slower. You can come in here every ten years and clean out infestations of Florida holly and keep it under control, but soda apple—in a matter of a couple of years it can take over entire areas in and around the oak hammocks. Living here and working here all the time, you quickly learn where it's at and keep after it. You know to go out at certain times of the year, send people out, and keep it under control.

RAY: We're hoping that when the state takes over, they won't just let it sit and grow back into a jungle. The state is realizing that they have a responsibility to the public to not only buy these kinds of properties but to properly maintain them.

JOURNALIST: What have you enjoyed most about living and working here?

STEVE: Just the joy of having the place. Having access to such a unique piece of property has always struck me as being very fortunate. It's a unique experience that most people don't have. I won't have access like I have now, the freedom to go do what I want. It is somewhat of a comfort to know that it's going to be preserved as opposed to selling it to a developer and watching a bunch of houses go up out here. There is some comfort in that.

JOURNALIST: Where will you go from here?

STEVE: After we dry our tears, we may have to go into town and get jobs. Ray and I will get to keep part of the property for our homes. Maybe we can work for the state to help manage it.

Although I was prepared to camp, the brothers offered for me to stay in their grandfather's rustic fishing and hunting cabin on the wild shores of Lake Istokpoga. Ray gave me a map of the property, showing me the location of the cabin, natural features, and places to hike. He mentioned that the western edge of the property had been a boundary for a Seminole Indian reservation in the early 1800s. He also explained that the property had a high level of biodiversity because of habitat types that range from desertlike scrub to freshwater wetlands. "Now it's going to be wet out there," he cautioned. "We just had a tropical storm that dumped several inches of rain."

Just my luck, I thought. Here I was in the driest part of Florida in terms of annual rainfall, and I visit during a flood.

The cabin was a welcome surprise. It was cypress-sided and tin-roofed, with enfolding arms of live oak trees framing it perfectly. From the screened porch, I had a commanding view of Lake Istokpoga.

Inside, deer antlers and a rattlesnake skin lined the walls. A rust-encrusted wood stove was still operational along with an antique cupboard and ice cooler. The utensils and furnishings were vintage 1940s. Unintentionally, a backwoods museum.

The rustic cabin triggered a type of frontier memory for me—aromas of natural wood and past fires, a sense of relaxation when crossing the weathered threshold, a feeling of basic living near virgin lands. If my job were to simply chronicle a backwoods cabin stay, it would have been easy. But my task was to write about and photograph the property's natural features, and that meant getting outside and swimming if I had to.

From the cabin, I embarked on a long loop hike on what was supposed to be dry trail. I soon began wading knee-deep in water and muck with my camera tripod serving as a staff to keep me upright. My free hand swatted thousands of newly hatched mosquitoes. The welcoming committee. I inhaled mosquitoes, exhaled mosquitoes, and swallowed mosquitoes—extra protein. I splashed on repellent, but quickly sweated it off. Despite the heat and clear skies, I scrambled to put on a blue hooded raincoat. I zipped it up tight. The foolhardiness of my hiking endeavor was not lost upon me. I asked myself the proverbial question: What was I doing? Most sane people would never have left the cabin.

The reward for my wet slogging was wildlife. I interrupted two feeding raccoons near the lake. They scurried up a cypress tree, only to peer curiously from a branch. A medium-sized indigo snake slithered past. It, too, paused to look at me. I must have been a strange sight—a blue man.

I stopped before an aged deer carcass. It looked as though a large animal had dragged it out of a cypress swamp to finish it off. I couldn't see anything in the dark swamp but wondered if more animal eyes were upon me—hidden, watching eyes, perhaps those of a black bear or even a panther.

As the hardwood hammock that I traversed gave way to wet prairie and open slash pine forest, I heard the unmistakable cry of a Florida sandhill crane. Aptly described by ornithologists as a loud "rolling croak," the sandhill's call struck me as an auditory signal of wildness in peninsular Florida, much like the roar of an alligator or the almost forgotten scream of a Florida panther. Only about four thousand of the tall, graceful birds remain in the state, and protected areas of shallow wetlands and adjacent uplands are vital to their survival.

I searched for the cranes, soon spotting two of them in a clearing. I quietly approached, aiming my camera. "Brrrruuh!" A deep-throated grunt emerged from a nearby pine thicket. "Brrruuh!" I heard it again. I froze. Mysterious grunts always have a chilling effect.

I peered into shadows and made out a massive wild hog with piglets. The two cranes slowly edged away; I sought to follow their example. If there was any dangerous critter in these woods, it would be a riled-up mother hog. I stepped back. The hog grunted louder. Freezing again, I glanced around for possible trees to climb, spotting only tall pines that lacked lower limbs. Perhaps my tripod and camera could serve as a weapon, I thought.

I inched back more slowly; the hog stopped grunting. I made a wide arc around the beast, scaring up several white-tailed deer and a wild turkey. Silver Harbor was living up to its reputation as a wildlife haven.

If I had a gun, I could have shot my limit, but I was hunting with a camera. Plus, I worried about growing darkness. The wet conditions had slowed my progress; I had underestimated the time it would take to slog three miles—three hours instead of one. I focused on the cabin, directing my wet legs to take me there.

From the cabin, I could find refuge from mosquitoes. I could dry off and change clothes. I would have no worries of boars or other beasts. I could artificially keep the night away, but still let in rhythmic sounds— frogs, insects, and owl. The cabin's lights and windows would allow me to adjust my exposure, and I could distract myself with books.

From the cabin, I could also look forward to morning and full light, when I planned to search for bald eagles, Sherman's fox squirrels, gopher tortoises, wood storks, Florida scrub jays, and sand skinks, all threatened or endangered species found on the property. I could explore a rare habitat known as the cutthroat grass seep, named for a very localized species of grass that thrives where water seeps out of

Fig. 19. Dale Allen paddles a windy Lake Hatchineha.

pine sandhills. I could search for the equally rare wedge-leaved button snakeroot that grows there.

Maybe I would visit a large, intact Native American mound on the property, and ponder those the archaeologists call the Deptford people, who flourished in these parts about two thousand years ago. Excavations revealed clues to an extensive trade network with other native people in eastern North America. I would ponder how they lived, what they ate, and, more importantly, how they viewed the universe. Like the cabin, their huts and villages were refuges, bases from which to interact with the broader world.

The woods were shadowy; trees appeared more as dark shapes against a purple western sky. The cabin, I thought, where was the cabin? A half hour before, I was certain I was following the right direction. Now, I wasn't so sure. A prickly feeling of panic enveloped me. To spend the night here, in the wild, with no light, no fire—only mosquitoes and loud grunts and mud and water—wasn't appealing. I had to find the cabin!

I came upon a familiar muddy road and eagerly followed it toward the lakeshore, entering a grove of twisted live oaks. Relieved, I breathed more deeply. Standing before the rustic cabin in the dim light was a human form. I had company. The closer I came, the more I made out a Seminole Indian man with gray hair and an old style patchwork long coat. He smiled as I approached; he had a kind face. I nodded to him. Maybe he had helped in some way, I thought. Reaching the door, I fumbled for the light switch while the apparition faded into the Istokpoga night.

Luckily, there was still plenty of daylight as we surfed across Lake Hatchineha, pushed by a stiff breeze that was whipping up whitecaps. I was swept into the open water so quickly by the wind that I didn't even have time to put on my spray skirt. The skirt serves to keep water out of the hatch and thus can prevent the kayak from swamping. Turning toward the C-37 Canal exposed us to the wind broadside, making me more nervous, but everyone made it safely across. The C-37 connects lakes Hatchineha and Kissimmee. Once paddling in the more protected waters of the canal, we made our way to Camp Mack, an old-time fish camp with plenty of mosquitoes. Everyone's muscles were a bit sore, but hot showers and a good dinner picked us all up. It was our longest day yet—about thirteen miles.

chapter 4

Fish Camps and Airboats

Camp Mack resembled several other fish camps along the route. It consisted of docks and a ramp, numerous boats, a small store, and rustic outbuildings nestled under arching live oak trees, a big American flag, and lots of pickup trucks and camper trailers.

At Camp Mack, perched on the edge of a side canal in between lakes Hatchineha and Kissimmee, fishermen and hunters sat around a smoldering fire in front of the camp store day and night, swapping stories and listening to country music. The campers there had never seen kayakers along the chain of lakes. Airboats and other motorized crafts were the more common modes of water travel.

Fishing and hunting were the main focus at Camp Mack and other Kissimmee camps; the entire chain of lakes is renowned for its bass and panfish fishing. Newspaper accounts, such as the one quoted below from the 1882 *New Orleans Times-Democrat* expedition, helped to spread the word about the legendary fishing. In this passage, the crew fished the natural passageway leading south from Lake Toho to Cypress Lake:

> Capt. Andrews, wishing to try the excellence of a new "spinner," among the fish, we get in one of the boats and row down the river, with the "spinner" glistening in the water, which is as clear as crystal, about 10 yards from the stern of our boat. "Stand from under," yells Capt. Andrews, and looking behind, I witness for the first time in my life, the fight for his life, of the

gamest fish which swims to-wit: The black bass. Darting from side to side, the line cutting through the water like a knife, never allowing it to slacken for a second, he is hauled to the side of the boat, and the captain his face red from the exertion, and his fingers tingling from the cutting of the line, lands safely in the bottom of the boat our first fish of the expedition, which we find, upon putting him in the scales, weighs just ten and a quarter pounds. . . . Another and another is hauled over our gunwale, until we begin to feel the fish must be a foot thick at the bottom of the river. As I step from the boat to the shore, I feel for the first time in my life, I have had half an hour of such fishing as I have often heard, and read of, but never seen or experienced. In one short half hour, by actual weight, with one single line, we had caught 108 pounds of fish.

Fig. 20. Camp Mack storefront. The fish camp was the destination for day four. Photo by Bob Mindick.

That evening, the expedition enjoyed the flavor of fried, broiled, baked and stewed bass, prepared by the party's chef.

Regarding hunting, the 1882 expedition frequently shot ducks and other animals from their boats. In one account, when they didn't have a dog to retrieve fallen ducks, they took advantage of their overworked African American cook:

"Here comes a flock of ducks," says the Colonel, in an excited tone, and in a second both he and myself, with guns in hand, the men resting on their oars, are gazing at a large flock of mallards coming right toward us. Nearer and nearer they come, and when within 20 yards we fire together, both of us emptying both barrels of our guns ere we cease. The splashing in the water of the wounded ducks in the marsh tell us we have bagged some. The Colonel says he is certain we have killed at least 20, and I am more certain we have killed 30. The high marsh grass covered with water "hide our game" from view. We have no water dog to bring it to us, so we give Caesar, our cook a dose of "antidote for snake bite," and tumble him overboard. We hear him splashing around in the marsh and in about 10 minutes he reappears with one duck. He says it is all he can find, and we begin using some very polite language to him. In fact, we insinuated that he never descended from any of George Washington's old family servants, etc. We give him another drink, as his teeth are chattering like castanets, and send him back. Another 10 minutes pass, and back he comes with two more, which he swears are all. We don't believe him, haul out the bottle, and send him back grinning again. Five minutes more, and two more ducks are added to the pile. Caesar looks serious, as we again haul out the bottle and insist on one more search. Once more he primes himself against snake bites, and is rewarded by a single duck. Either Caesar has had enough to drink, there are no more ducks, or he don't want the bother of cooking and cleaning any more, for no persuasion can induce him to try it again, so we haul him aboard and continue our course.

Fig. 21. Jerry Renney, longtime environmental activist for Kissimmee restoration and public access, serenades the group at Camp Mack.

The "antidote for snakebite" was a new concoction of the time, an 1882 oral version of antivenin shots, and no one on the trip needed to test its effectiveness.

On our journey, venomous snakes were not a problem, but we did have encounters with curious dogs. When Beth went on a short walking tour of Camp Mack, she returned to loud shouts and serious laughter from our camp area. A dog had walked up to her water sandals by her tent and started to raise his leg to relieve himself. At that point, everybody started yelling and gesticulating, and the freaked-out dog ran for his life. "The moral of the story is that it is time to wash my water sandals!" Beth remarked.

Jerry Renney serenaded us with song at Camp Mack. Jerry was an early activist with the Kissimmee River Valley Sportsman's Association, fighting for public access to area waters and trying to clean up and restore the river system. His songs were passionate, nostalgic, and heartwarming, sometimes about "when Florida could make you feel small." It can still make visitors feel small, especially in parts of the Kissimmee valley.

Many of the sovereign rights conflicts of the 1980s—mostly with ranchers who were blocking access to some of the lakes—were resolved when the South Florida Water Management District simply bought the land or acquired easements instead of fighting lengthy and expensive court battles. Jerry concluded, "What's happened here in my home, the Kissimmee River valley, has made it a whole lot better than it used to be." These positive developments created a dilemma for Jerry: "It's hard to be an activist without a cause," he chuckled.

After a song about his love for traveling the waters in his airboat, Jerry concluded: "Hey, I've got a joke for you. What do you call kayaks if you're in an airboat? . . . Speed bumps."

We had entered the heart of airboat country—from here to Florida Bay. Even conservation activists such as Jerry Renney drove airboats. An anthropologist could argue that airboat users are part of a distinct subculture, an independent breed that takes pride in assembling the boats themselves, often with used and salvaged parts and motors. They also repair them in the field when they are miles from the nearest shop. "The airboat is peculiarly their thing," said author Stuart B. McIver, "a gritty, common-sense, down-to-earth-and-water contraption born of Depression necessity."

The first airboat prototype was built by inventor Alexander Graham Bell and aviation pioneer and designer Glenn Curtiss around 1905. It was a motorboat equipped with aerial propellers mounted in the bow that pulled the boat much like a prop propeller. "We have named her the Ugly Duckling and hope she will turn out to be a swan," wrote Bell at the time.

Curtiss later moved to South Florida and founded Opa-Locka. He invented an aerodynamic craft with a rear-mounted aircraft engine that pushed the boat across the water and marsh much like today's airboats. His first boat could fit a half dozen people and move up to 50 miles per hour. A smaller craft he built reached speeds up to 70 miles per hour.

A few years later, unaware of Curtiss's efforts, a couple of Everglades frog hunters created two crude airboats using automobile engines that traveled 8 to 10 miles per hour. Improvements were made

Fig. 22. Dale Allen, Beth Kelso, and Mike Jones lead off the hiking contingent of the group on day five.

over time, such as a high seat, steering stick, and gas pedal. Now new strides are being made to make airboats run more quietly—with mufflers and new propeller designs—while keeping the features that allow the craft to maneuver in shallow and marshy areas. There will likely never be such a thing as a quiet airboat, however, unless it is running at a very low speed or not running at all. To push air at enough velocity to move a heavy boat will inevitably produce a noise that is displeasing to some.

Since we were camping adjacent to the boat ramp at Camp Mack, we were frequently awakened by airboats being launched and started up with a roar in the wee hours. Many of the men were turkey hunters dressed in camo wanting to reach their favorite hunting spots well before sunrise. It was like trying to sleep beside a runway for prop planes, with the exhaust fumes to go with it.

Around 4 A.M., an airboat engine fired and then sputtered to a halt. "Hey, Doug!" a man yelled in the darkness, "I'll go get that tool.

Hang on!" Hearing my name jolted me awake, even though the man was calling a different Doug. I could hear the clanking of wrenches while someone started tinkering with the engine. The next sounds were those of grunting men as they inexplicably loaded a squealing pig onto the airboat. A minute later, the engine roared to life again and the airboat slowly faded into the Kissimmee night. Even though we enjoyed several aspects of fish camp life such as the scenic live oaks, showers, store, and friendly people, the nightly noise pointed out the need for a primitive campsite in the area, where paddlers could sleep uninterrupted.

Camp Mack marked the spot where half the group began hiking to Lake Okeechobee—scouting a potential footpath that would link up to the Florida Trail—while the other half continued kayaking. I stayed with the kayakers. We were to meet the hikers every night at a prearranged campsite.

chapter 5

Lake Kissimmee Challenges

Crossing the massive 35,000-acre Lake Kissimmee, we hit open stretches where two- to three-foot waves crashed over our bows. The east wind hadn't let up since day one, and, having popped out on the northwest end of the lake, we were bearing the full brunt of its force.

The east wind had special meaning to my adopted Muskogee Creek uncle, Bear Heart. Bear Heart was a member of the Wind Clan, part of a lineage passed down through his mother's side. It is believed that members of the same clan are related, one reason that traditional native people do not marry within their own clan. Most clans have a kinship with certain animal species, but Wind Clan people have a special kinship with the wind.

Learned in the medicine ways of his people, Bear Heart was a healer, and more than once I had been the recipient of his talents. When he fanned me with a special feather from his medicine box, often one from an eagle, it felt like a warm electrifying wind coursing through my body. Don't ask me to explain. In my mind, it's all part of the "Great Mystery."

Regarding the wind, Bearheart told me that the east wind was a medicine wind, a healing wind. On our trip, the east wind had blown unceasingly for six straight days, perhaps not as much a medicine wind for us as for the lakes and streams of the Kissimmee valley. For a paddler, the wind can caress and challenge, nurture and punish, sometimes all in the same day.

Fig. 23. Bob Mindick nears the entrance to Lake Kissimmee; the hazy fog made it appear that he was paddling off the end of the earth.

Archie Williams, in 1882, described Lake Kissimmee's vastness, and the wind:

> As far as the eye can reach in a southerly direction, even with glasses, we are unable to discern any land, nothing meeting the view but a wide expanse of water. A stiff norther is blowing, and the whitecaps of the waves remind us more of salt water than that of an inland lake.

At one point, Bob lost his paddle in the choppy water. He had hooked it to the side of his craft so he could use his bicycle apparatus, but he had failed to secure the paddle to the kayak with what is known as a paddle leash. Waves had evidently knocked it loose. We backtracked to search for the lost paddle in the waves and whitecaps but failed to find it. I wondered what an angler would do with a kayak paddle should he or she come across it. Fortunately, like most prepared kayakers, Bob brought a spare.

It's funny how certain situations or incidents will trigger memories. The last time I had tried to paddle across such a large lake, I was sixteen years old. I had accompanied my older brother, David, and two friends on an ambitious attempt to canoe the entire Mississippi River, beginning at Lake Itasca, Minnesota. We had two canoes with front seats that were farther back than normal so that someone could sleep in the front at night while his partner paddled. We left tents at home. Paddling day and night was the only way we could finish the 2,500-mile journey before school started at the end of August and before we ran out of money. The idea had sounded fine in our heads, but in practice, bugs, rapids, fog, and storms made sleeping or paddling in the dark nearly impossible.

On the night of day three, my "sleep" shift started at midnight, and I was finally able to conk out from exhaustion, having had little sleep for three days. Two hours later, Ken, my partner, screamed for me to wake up: "Paddle! Paddle!" Bleary-eyed, I popped up my head to see a raging sea with no land in sight. We were crossing the 58,544-acre Lake Winnibigoshish, created by a dam on the river, and a thunderstorm was just about to strike. Lightning flashed across the dark sky ahead and ominous thunder boomed.

I grabbed my wooden paddle and joined in the effort against a mighty headwind. Rain began pelting us. The front of the canoe rose high and crashed down hard, spraying water. "Kneel in the front!" Ken shouted. "There's too much weight in the back." I did as instructed, and we paddled mightily against the storm and waves. A mixture of fear and adrenalin fueled our efforts. Our muscles burned.

At the first light of dawn, we gave up, the distant shoreline still miles away. The wind had won. Exhausted, we retreated to the south shore and spent the day paddling a more indirect route around the huge lake. That's when I told the group that, according to my calculations, we couldn't make it to the Gulf of Mexico before school started. In my head, I was also saying that I couldn't make it to the distant Gulf. I don't think any of us could have with the ill-fated plan we had concocted. We quit soon after leaving the lake and tried to make our way home with low funds and a gas-guzzling U-Haul truck. That was another adventure altogether. To his credit, Ken returned to Minnesota the following spring—with a tent for camping every night—and paddled the entire Mississippi River in a little over two months. I stayed home.

Fortunately, on Lake Kissimmee, it was daylight and not storming, and we wisely decided to hug the shore behind a line of marsh, pickerel weed, duck potato, and lily pads that buffered the waves. Midges—small mosquitolike insects that swarm but don't bite—were prevalent. Locals call them "chizzy winks." I had to be careful when opening my mouth or I would inhale them. "They are attracted to the minerals on your skin," said Bob. Swallows swooped and dove to feed on the midges. Also in the marshes were fishermen in boats who had gathered in clusters to fish for speckled perch. Their bent poles made it apparent that the fish were biting.

Lake Kissimmee is almost completely undeveloped and rich with bird life. I paused near the shore at one point and observed a crested caracara strolling among cattle. This threatened bird of prey with the unmistakable black hood has strong legs that enable it to easily walk or run on the ground, opportunistically feeding on small mammals, reptiles, amphibians, and carrion. A flock of glossy ibis flew past— black silhouettes against the sky. Then I spotted wild turkeys walking across the pasture. They came to the water's edge and poked up their heads for a look at me in a reciprocal expression of curiosity. They were all hens, I determined, since their brown bodies lacked the crimson markings of tom turkeys.

As we continued south past mats of lily pads, wading birds cried and poked around the shallows. Brown and gray blue snail kites, a federally designated endangered species, swooped through tall marsh grass from hidden nests while raptors filled the skies—eagle, osprey, and swallowtail kite.

The water weeds, coupled with the humid air, put off a wild, sweet aroma that told me I was along a freshwater shore. My first memory was the refreshing scent of lakeside willow, and so this place reminded me of my beginning. The smell of life!

Bob and I were the first to pull into a fish camp on the lake's western shore. It was marked by a decrepit pier that seemed to have weathered one too many hurricanes. Ian was close behind. This was our planned destination for the night. As we walked up to the dilapidated buildings, escaping the wind's embrace, the midges and heat became stifling. The place was empty of people except for a friendly bearded man whose size brought to mind someone who could wrestle a large

Fig. 24. An osprey at Lake Kissimmee. Photo by Bob Mindick.

Fig. 25. A snail kite, an endangered species, perched along Lake Kissimmee. The kite primarily feeds on apple snails that live in marshes with long hydroperiods. Photo by Bob Mindick.

gator, and maybe he had. He was wearing overalls and a gold chain that seemed out of place until I recognized the tiny gold object that dangled on the end of the sparkling necklace—an airboat.

Bob and I knocked on the door of the main house to check in. A man's gravelly voice told us to enter. A strong odor of fried food hit my nostrils, and I realized it had been several days since I had set foot in a house. I felt awkward.

A gray-haired man nodded a greeting and shook our hands. He was expecting us. He then said, "I've been feeling real sick lately. Flu or something going around." Knowing it was impolite to immediately wash my hand, I shoved it into my pocket. We were at the halfway point of the trip, and the idea of kayaking the next several days with flu symptoms wasn't appealing.

"So, how many are coming in for the night?" the man asked.

"Seven, plus a couple more in vehicles," Bob replied, "and a documentary film crew of three. They've got a couple of tents, so there's maybe ten tents in all."

The man sighed. "I know my wife quoted you a price on the phone," he began, "but it wasn't right. It's thirty-five dollars a tent. You can camp anywhere."

Bob glanced at me with raised eyebrows, trying to conceal a smirk. "Thirty-five dollars a tent—that's a little steep," he protested. "Only the film crew might want electricity." The quoted price had been $17.50 a tent, and I thought even that was steep, considering the unkempt appearance of the camp and its lack of shade.

"Thirty-five dollars it is," the man replied. "I'm sorry she told you the wrong information on the phone."

"We'll need to talk it over with the others," Bob replied, refusing to lay down any money. We exited the house. Once outside, Bob said: "He knows he has us over a barrel. He figures on making as much as he can." I wondered if the owner's attitude had contributed to the near-total lack of customers at the camp.

"I think I'll go for a walk and try to meet the hikers coming in," I said. "Plus, I need to get out of these midges." One nearby white truck appeared to be dark gray, its surface covered with thousands of the bugs.

I found an old road through an oak hammock and headed north, hoping to meet the hikers head-on. After walking for a couple of miles with no sign of them, I turned around, figuring they had taken a route closer to the lake shore. When I reached the camp, to my surprise, I spotted the documentary crew headed out into the windy lake, their motorboat piled high with gear. Bill Graf, the South Florida Water Management District media liaison, approached me and explained what happened, "There's been a group insurrection," he said. "When the hikers came in and found out about the doubling of camping fees, they wouldn't stand for it. We made a call and received permission from the owners of nearby Brahma Island to stay at their hunting cabin. It's about seven more miles to their landing on the other side of the island." He showed me the spot on a map.

My head was whirling—seven more miles! And the wind had increased in velocity. Ian had waited for me in his kayak. Bob had understandably left as soon as the vote was cast. His boat was slower, and he is diabetic.

By his frown, I knew Ian was perturbed. The hikers would ride to the island in a motorboat after they finished walking three more miles to another rendezvous point, but the paddlers had to deal with the vicious headwind. I had counted on eating a late lunch, and maybe take a rare nap, but I quickly threw gear into my hatches, slipped on my spray skirt, strapped on my life jacket, and gobbled downed a granola bar.

"Who's the leader of this expedition anyway?" Ian asked when we embarked. Ian was a latecomer to the team and wasn't part of our organizational meetings.

"No one," I said. "We decided we were going to decide things as a group."

"Figures," he grumbled. After twenty years of taking and giving orders in the army, he was more accustomed to a chain of command. I gathered that the decision to leave the fish camp was made hastily, and without everyone's full input. There had been a quick vote, and the majority ruled.

Ian soon shot out ahead. He had to work out some frustration about whatever had transpired, I figured. I still felt dazed at the change of events, and suddenly famished. I felt alone, the unrelenting wind whistling in my ears. My muscles burned, but I couldn't stop or I'd be blown backward. I vowed not give up like on the Upper Mississippi River and lakes. Overall, our planning had been good. The wind howled, but it hadn't stormed, and the group was generally compatible and fun-loving.

When I reached the other side of the massive 4,000-acre island, I caught up with Bob. We commiserated about the fish camp owner, the wind, and our weariness. Our somber mood was briefly broken by the hikers as they roared past in the motorboat on their way to the island dock. They screamed their greeting, and Beth shot us a moon. The flash of pale buttocks rocking up and down with the boat added

Fig. 26. Brahma Island live oaks. Photo by Bob Mindick.

a surreal quality to our situation. Then we were alone again with the wind and waves.

Once settled in the rustic hunting cabin, the good humor of the group prevailed. We had hot showers, full kitchen facilities, and a rickety pool table that needed leveling. It made the games more fun. Ian and Mike returned to telling military jokes—"Why do the navy guys enjoy having marines on board ship? . . . Because they have more dance partners." It was summer camp for adults.

Our hosts, Cary and Layne Lightsey, gave us a warm welcome. "I've stayed in cow camps all my life," said Cary, "so I appreciate a shower and the better things in life."

Virginia, the news anchorwoman, tried to describe the rigors of camping out every night to Cary, but she got some of the words mixed up: "The worst part about this wild living is not the alligators or the wild whores—I mean boars—it's the red ants. They're mean!"

Walls of the cabin were liberally decorated with the heads of slain animals—mostly wild hogs—along with rattlesnake skins. Photos, too, were numerous, such as ones of visiting celebrities such as Johnny Depp and Shaq. Shaq, the seven-foot-one, three-hundred-pound basketball center, needed two bunks end to end to fit his massive body. And the Lightseys described Depp as "quiet and real respectful." Also present were numerous rifles and boxes of ammunition. You wouldn't expect anything less from a hunting cabin.

We were surrounded by 4,000 acres of uninhabited island. We felt like the luckiest people alive.

chapter 6

"We're Just Running Cows Here Instead of Building Homes"

Cary Lightsey, slim, mustached, and sandy-haired, led us on a driving tour down sugar-sand roads beneath canopies of arching live oaks, passing a sign that read: "Do Not Shoot Trees." It seemed that every time we passed an opening or glimpsed the sky or treetops, we spotted eagles. They were perched, circling, or swooping over the lake or dry prairies. Lightsey often tilted back his cowboy hat and pointed to an eagle, in case we missed it. "Seeing an eagle puts a smile on my face," he said. He must smile a lot, I thought. Up to one hundred eagles have been counted on the island at one time, one of the highest concentrations of nonmigratory bald eagles in the lower forty-eight states.

Lightsey was also quick to point out that twenty-eight protected species call Brahma Island home, an incredibly high number that he says enhances the value of the land. Did I say that we found his attitude refreshing?

Many of the massive oaks we visited were bent and twisted from past hurricanes. Some were nearly four hundred years old—the oldest in peninsular Florida. They were mature even when Zachary Taylor drove Seminole Indians off the island in 1837 during the Second Seminole War. One battered oak was estimated to have fallen from hurricane force winds eight times, and it was struck by lightning at least twice.

Fig. 27. Cary Lightsey guides news anchorwoman Virginia Johnson and other team members on a jeep tour of Brahma Island.

Lightsey, a sixth-generation Florida cattle rancher, and his family sold most of their development rights to the state so future generations of Lightseys can carry on the family business without selling the land to developers. "They [water management district officials] come once a year to make sure we're not upsetting the land any, cutting timber or doing anything we're not supposed to. It's just that simple. We're just running cows here instead of building homes. It's a win-win for us because we get to keep doing what we love to do, and what we love to do is to get on a horse with our kids and grandkids and work cattle every day and enjoy our wildlife and enjoy our green space, and knowing that we're providing a recharge area for the citizens of the state.

"If you are a rancher who cares about your heritage, you want your children to stay in this business. We're fortunate to be in an area where the state has come in and bought most everybody out. And I'd like to say that if it wasn't for the large ranchers on these chain of lakes to Lake Okeechobee, this land would have been developed a long

Fig. 28. Some of the weathered live oaks on Brahma Island are more than four hundred years old.

time ago. These are bona-fide ranchers who wanted to keep ranching on the best cow land in the state of Florida, and so they didn't want to develop either. There are a big percentage of people that's jumping on the bandwagon that wants to do these easements [selling development rights to the state]."

For Lightsey and others like him, ranching is the only thing they have known. His family started raising cattle in North America in 1712. After John Lightsey fought Seminoles in 1837, he eventually packed up his family and moved to the Kissimmee valley from Georgia in 1858, driving their cattle with them. They've been cracking whips under the Florida sun ever since. "My Dad had a story he always told us—if you were a Lightsey and you was taken away from your family as a young person and moved to another state, you'd go in the cattle business. It's in our blood." He chuckled, rubbing a leathery face.

He described how Lake Kissimmee changed when the Kissimmee River was canalized and the locks and dams were built in the 1960s. "The shoreline and lake bottom used to be very sandy and open," he said, "but then it began to silt up, and the cattails and maidencane and other plants came in, and when they decomposed, they contributed to the siltation." He fully supports the restoration efforts. "We think that eventually it's going to go back to that [a more natural state]. We think we can get the lows and highs and probably get the land to being cleaner."

The Lightsey family, like others who settled in the Kissimmee valley in the 1800s, quickly learned that the fertile land could support a high number of grazing animals. And with wild Spanish scrub cattle for the taking, some early immigrants with only a few dollars in their pockets eventually became rich cattle barons. Cuban buyers paid up to fifteen dollars a head in gold doubloons. Cattle were marked with distinctive brands or earmarks, and rounded up and driven to the southwest Florida coast to towns such as Punta Rassa and Punta Gorda, where they were sold and loaded onto boats headed for Cuba and other Latin countries.

During the Civil War, Florida became a major supplier of beef for the Confederate army. In 1863, with food supplies dwindling, several Floridians serving in the Confederate army were allowed to return home to round up and drive cattle north. Besides dealing with constant threats from Union "rustlers" from St. Augustine and elsewhere, the "Cow Cavalry," as they were called, had to deal with desperate deserters and outlaws. "The Cow Cavalry not only tried to protect every one of the scrawny Florida scrub cows," writes Jim Robison in *Kissimmee: Gateway to the Kissimmee Valley*, "but scattered units also raided Union troops up and down the St. Johns River. The Confederate government had organized the cattleman cavalry from some rough characters, cow hunters, ranchers, and settlers."

Even during the Civil War, some cattlemen still sold beef to the Cubans along the southwest coast since they received a higher price than what the Confederacy paid, and this trade resumed full force after the war.

The cow hunter of the 1800s lived a rough life, often using a tin can for cooking, a saddle for a pillow, and smudge fires to discourage mosquitoes. Frequently, he had to deal with rattlesnakes and wild animals, and sometimes with floods and hurricanes.

Cow hunters employed a small but tough horse known as a "marsh tackie." The early Spanish breed had adapted well to Florida's environment; they were renowned for their endurance and ability to maneuver through marshes and thick vegetation. Cow hunter dogs were equally tough. The cur dogs could run down an errant cow in the scrub and clamp on the animal's nose until the cow hunter arrived.

The gaunt cattle the Florida wrangler hunted, marked, and tried to herd were descendents of Spanish Andalusian cattle and British colonial breeds introduced decades and centuries earlier. Well adapted to the insects, tropical heat, and often sparse native forage of the Florida wilderness, they could be as wild as deer and highly uncooperative.

A famous story of a feisty bull named Old Frostysides was told by Captain Francis Asbury Hendry, who drove herds in the Fort Meade area in the 1870s. Hendry's account was published in *Cracker: The Cracker Culture in Florida History*, by Dana Ste. Claire:

> Just as I was a-turnin the p'int of the bayhead, Old Frosty come out of that swamp like a tornado, with a great load of vines around his horns. I spurred Jack and squared myself before him. Then I give him a few right smart cracks with my drag, tryin to turn him into the herd, but he kept comin for me full tilt. Back of me was a

p'int of sawgrass, and there wasn't no way to run ' cept into that bog. The old fool steer by this time had his long horns very near Jack's kickin' end. Jack must known it was boggy in that slough, cause he stopped sudden and fell to kickin.' Me and Jack parted company quicker than lightnin,' and left me and Old Frosty to settle the dispute between ourselves. . . . [T]he first thing I seen when I raised up out of the mud was Old Frosty's eyes looking green at me, his tongue out, with ropes of slobber streamin from his mouth and nostrils. He was all set to run me through . . . how I did it, I don't know, but I snatched my hat off and swung it at him. The p'int of one horn stuck right through the crown, and rested square over Old Frosty's eyes so he couldn't see a thing. I guess it's still there yet, and I hope it'll rot there.

Stampedes were a threat that Florida cow hunters shared with their western counterparts, although the aftermath of a stampede witnessed by the black cowman Lawrence Silas of Osceola County in the early 1900s was likely never seen in the West, nor since in Florida. "Eleven hundred steers went into a stampede," he began, his words recorded in Ste. Claire's book. "We men heard it in time and run in every direction. The stampede headed for a big swamp. Wasn't a thing we could do. The next morning we followed the trail down to the edge of the swamp. We knowed that the ground was too soft for ' em to get across. They didn't, you couldn't see no cows at all. All you could see was horns, just a whole lake of horns."

Morgan Bonaparte "Bone" Mizell was perhaps the most legendary of the early Florida cow hunters, known for his abilities and exploits on and off the job. One story has him catching an ornery unmarked cow in the brush by hand and making his own mark on the poor animal's ears with his teeth. Another tale describes how he tried to obtain a marriage license while drinking, but he couldn't remember the lucky girl's name.

Friends would often take advantage of Bone after he had passed out from drinking. It was said that they wished to scare him into quitting or moderating his habit, but they probably got a good laugh out of it, too. Once Bone was placed in a coffin with the top nailed shut and sent on a train heading north. Upon awakening, he began to scream and flail his arms and legs, thinking that he had been buried alive. A surprised conductor freed him.

On another occasion, Bone awoke to fire burning all around him, upon which he is said to have exclaimed, "I am in hell!" Friends had piled a circle of dried cow chips around his sleeping body and lit the flammable ring just before dawn.

So popular was the colorful Bone that after he was sentenced to two years in the state penitentiary for misbranding calves—a common but unlawful practice in which a calf was given a different brand than the mother cow—friends immediately pushed for his pardon. A petition drive gained widespread support. The judge who sentenced him declared that a pardon couldn't be granted until Bone had spent some time in prison. So Bone was presented with a new suit and sent off to prison to the music of the town band. Upon arriving at the state penitentiary, Bone was given a celebrity-style tour and banquet. Having completed his "sentence," he was handed a pardon and sent home on the return train.

Other illegal activities during the era were not greeted with such indulgence. Rustling and range wars sometimes occurred, especially in the vast piney woods west of the Kissimmee valley; lawmen were rarely called in to settle disputes. Wealthy owners fielded heavily armed outfits, and the thick forests and swamps easily concealed the aftermath of a battle or ambush. Surviving perpetrators could conveniently escape into the Everglades, following the example of fleeing Seminoles. When affairs were brought to court, the armed contingent of men in the courtroom would generally ensure a compromise decision.

Trains would frequently kill open-range cattle, and owners would then demand an often inflated and immediate recompense. A delay in payment might result in the lanterns of a passing train being shot out, or worse. Such a "Winchester calling card" would usually speed up payment.

Cattle drives to Punta Gorda and Punta Rassa were often described as hell-raising affairs with some cow hunters quickly blowing hard-earned pay on drink and loose women. Shootings were commonplace, and storekeepers and bankers often wielded sawed-off shotguns and had their places of business heavily fortified to deter looters. One historian stated that in 1890s Arcadia, having fifty fights a day was commonplace and that four men were killed in one fight alone.

Kissimmee was a rough cattle town as well, but it had an advantage over the others. The town featured a ride-up saloon, a type of early take-out window where cowpokes could order and consume drinks while remaining on horseback. Plus, cowpokes could unload some of their weighty Spanish gold at a bona-fide horse track along Lake Tohopekaliga. The Wild West had nothing on Florida cattle towns.

After the Indian wars of the West died down, Florida was considered to be an untamed "last frontier" of the cowboy. This reputation lured the famous artist Frederic Remington to Florida's cattle country in 1895. Remington, bemoaning the fencing of rangeland west of the Mississippi, was sorely disappointed upon seeing Florida's open-range cowboys.

"Two very emaciated Texas ponies pattered down the street bearing wild-looking individuals," Remington wrote in "Cracker Cowboys of Florida," published by *Harper's* in 1895, "whose hanging hair and drooping hats and generally bedraggled appearance would remind you at once of the Spanish moss which hangs so quietly and helplessly to the limbs of oaks out in the swamps. . . . The only thing they did which were conventional were to tie their ponies up by the head in brutal disregard, and then get drunk in about 15 minutes."

Remington was shocked at the violence that could erupt over stealing wild Florida cattle. "Out in the wilderness low-browed cow folks shoot and stab each other for the possession of scrawny creatures not fit for a pointer-dog to mess on," he wrote. "The land gives only a tough wiregrass; and the poor little cattle, no bigger than a donkey, wander half-starved and horribly emaciated in search of it."

Such a description makes one wonder how early Florida cattlemen became so weighed down with Cuban gold, but it is safe to say that westerners like Remington were still grieving for the romanticized West they once knew and loved.

Remington didn't make it to the Kissimmee valley. If he did, he might have come away with a sense of appreciation for at least some of Florida's cattle country. "It was pretty well known that the Kissimmee valley was the ice-cream of grasses in Florida," said rancher Cary Lightsey. "There were very few people here in the middle 1800s. It was all open range, no fences. From about December 1 to when the rainy season started in July and August, people would drive their cattle here to the Kissimmee valley from hundreds of miles away. It was good grass—it had maidencane, broadleaf, all kinds of good marsh grasses. They would go ahead and burn the grass ahead of them, and this whole valley from Orlando to the Everglades was just thousands and thousands of head of cattle."

Ruby Jane Hancock, who grew up in the Kissimmee valley, described the early cattle operations of the 1800s in "The Kissimmee Valley: An Appreciation," published in *Tequesta* in 1979:

> The herders were paid in Spanish gold pieces. Having little to spend them on, when they returned home they threw these coarse sacks of coins up under the high wooden bedsteads where they slept with their wives. It is well to mention that locks to the valley houses were unheard of, but this gold was useless as tender in their primitive economy. Years later it was not uncommon to find holes dug around the early settlers' domains where people searched in hopes of finding buried gold, and the metal did become in many instances the capital for banks and other enterprises for the descendents of these early herders.

The early cattlemen had come to the valley in search of a new beginning. Many were army veterans, deserters, or drifters. In the isolated valley, men could obliterate their past and start fresh, and the land was large enough to take them all in. Hancock described the men and the culture that evolved around them:

> Outside of a shooting now and then, usually for good reasons, there was no crime of consequence in this isolated valley, and no formal legal justice was necessary. If one transgressed the unwritten code of mores and manners, he was quickly dispatched to the bottom of the river and forgotten. Verbal agreements were honored but not over handshakes, a custom not yet practiced by these independent folk, a "yep" or a "no" was sufficient, and if reneged, the fellow was treated like a pariah. Men were much like desert chieftains who had a peculiar comradeship at their cow camps and on the long drovin's to Punta Rassa; they

spent much time away from their homes and families. They were men of hearty appetites, good digestions, and sexual prowess but in general were faithful to their wives. They sat straight in their saddles, cracking their long hide whips, shooting their guns accurately, and could hold the strong whiskey they drank. But there were times when they left the woods and gathered their clans for barbecues, fish fries, and frolics, at the latter not missing a figure when the caller announced it.

A hurricane broke up the usual routines. Most of the herders lived in sturdy hand-hewn heart pine dwellings that withstood the storms, so taking care of the cattle and horses was of primary concern. Replanting gardens and repairing outbuildings would come later. Since many cattle would be marooned on Kissimmee River islands, they had to be driven to the mainland lest they starve. New calves and ponies would be rounded up and branded, and horses would have to be broken and trained for the annual cattle drives.

Other people in the valley included those who lived along and traveled the waterways, often called "river rats." Another group was the hardy Seminoles who had escaped removal, and who gradually developed a kinship with many of the isolated settlers. What all the people—river rats, ranchers, and Seminoles—had in common was the land and waters and the need for survival. For many decades leading into the twentieth century, before drainage and overhunting began to take their devastating toll, there was enough fish, game, and uninhabited territory to go around.

In time, cattle ranching changed, too. When railroads came to the lower Kissimmee valley in 1915, large herds of 1,000 to 1,200 cattle would be driven down Highway 98 or 441 through downtown Okeechobee to the railroad station. In the 1920s, the Cuban market declined, and since the Florida cattle did not compete as well for a share of the domestic market, other types of cattle were introduced. Fencing became more commonplace, open range was outlawed in 1949, and long cattle drives became a thing of the past.

The main threat to Kissimmee valley ranchers today is development that gobbles up land and alters their way of life forever. The

Kissimmee valley is at the center of what is increasingly referred to as Florida's Heartland—the largest undeveloped chunk of land remaining in peninsular Florida. Tempted by offers that approach twenty thousand dollars per acre for remote land, ranchers have begun selling their valuable spreads to developers and real estate speculators. Some are buying cheaper land in north Florida, Georgia, and Alabama in order to continue ranching. The developers, in turn, are being driven from the coasts by sky-high land prices and insurance costs, regulations, threats of hurricanes, and a lack of available property for large-scale developments.

Some of the largest development proposals are being touted as self-contained "new urbanist" communities. Florida is at the forefront of the new urbanism movement, with new towns sporting idealized names such as Seaside, Watercolor, Harmony, and Celebration. These communities are advertised as offering an environmentally friendly return to "Main Street" living, with viable downtown businesses and stores that allow residents to work, sleep, and shop within close proximity. Many neighborhoods boast a modified Cracker-style or coastal fishing village design, but without the rusty tin roofs and thrift-minded realities of yesteryear.

Most of the "pre-1940s," small-town–style homes for sale in Celebration, the first planned development of the Walt Disney Company near Kissimmee, were going for between $500,000 and $2 million each in 2008. Town homes and condos were selling for between $200,000 and $400,000. Celebration covers 4,900 acres, boasting a protected greenbelt of 4,700 acres, with a total investment of $2.5 billion. And the demand? In the original lottery in November 1995, five thousand people were vying for the first 350 lots.

Some environmentalists, believing that development is inevitable in Florida, embrace the concept of these planned communities, while others see them as further intrusions into vital wildlife habitats and traditional "Old Florida" ways of life. Along the Kissimmee valley, land around Lake Toho in Osceola County is seeing the most intense pressure. In 2008, no fewer than six large-scale residential developments were being proposed. Unlike in past years, however, shoreline buffers were being adopted along with special protections for eagle nests and for large trees that could be used by eagles in the future. In exchange for providing more open space, developers are usually allowed to build at a higher density.

On former ranch land near tiny Yeehaw Junction east of the Kissimmee River, the developer Anthony V. Pugliese III envisions a massive new urbanist community known as Destiny, with eighty thousand to one hundred thousand residents. "Destiny is going to be a special place for the young families, Baby Boomers and the Millennia Generation," he said in a 2006 investor blog. "We're going to be environmentally conscious, give people a place to get that pre-1940s feeling of kids skating on the street, parking your car in front of your house, walk to work and school, talk to your neighbors."

In a 2006 *St. Petersburg Times* article, Charles Lee, director of advocacy with Audubon of Florida, bluntly summarized his views regarding Destiny: "It pries open the interior of Florida like a can-opener."

In what has been touted as the biggest land deal since Walt Disney purchased his Orlando location for the "Magic Kingdom" in the mid-1960s, Pugliese bought the 27,410 acres for his Destiny dream town from the Latt Maxcy Cattle Corporation in 2005 for $137 million, easily outbidding state officials who were interested in purchasing the land for preservation. He hopes to lure a hospital and university research facilities to the property to help provide an economic engine for new residents. At the same time, he promises that about half the property will be set aside for conservation. Depending upon marketing and consumer demand, it will take between fifteen and forty years to build Destiny.

To service Destiny and other towns, and to help spawn new communities, powerbrokers have proposed two new toll roads—the north-south Heartland Parkway west of the Kissimmee River, and the east-west Heartland Coast-to-Coast. The proposed coast-to-coast road corridor skirts just south of the Avon Park Air Force Bombing Range and would span the restored section of the Kissimmee River. Proponents argue that if properly built, the roads offer unprecedented opportunities for conservation and transportation planning to go hand in hand. Opponents argue that they are roads to nowhere, bisecting

Fig. 29. Sunrise along the Shady Oaks campsite on Lake Kissimmee.

sensitive lands and helping a handful of large landowners and developers tap into a river of money.

In 2006, the proposed parkways seemed to be on a fast track. The Florida Department of Transportation had begun studying the proposals with little or no public input, spurred by then-governor Jeb Bush and a state senator who owned land along one of the corridors. But when Charlie Crist took over the governorship the next year, he advocated expanding existing roads instead of spending billions on new ones. His new secretary of the Department of Community Affairs, Tom Pelham, spoke directly to the Heartland toll road proposals in March 2007 in a *St. Petersburg Times* article. "Our concern is that we approach these from a comprehensive land planning perspective and then determine the appropriate transportation, not the reverse," he said. "Once transportation is locked in, that will be a magnet for development, and it will be too late."

For rancher Cary Lightsey and his family, keeping the land undeveloped along the Kissimmee valley is of paramount importance. "Florida has a very sensitive ecosystem," he said, pointing out that his family always left at least 40 percent of their land in native grasses and forest. "We're really just landlords of this land, if you really think about it. I feel like it's our job to protect it for the people of Florida."

chapter 7

The Kissimmee River

Maligned and Resurrected

Lake Kissimmee was a glassy calm as we left the lake from our shore-line campsite, contrasting with the waves and wind of the previous six days. We passed through a flood-control lock that marked the beginning of a long canal that was the channelized section of the Kissimmee River.

The Kissimmee—the translation of the early Native American word is disputed by scholars—was once a winding 103-mile natural waterway. John Rodgers, writing the introduction for the 1842 expedition account, reported it as "a deep, rapid stream, generally running through a marshy plain." But he also pointed out that, at certain points, pinelands and live oak hammocks fringed the channel.

The *Kissimmee Valley Gazette* in 1899 described the river as viewed from the deck of one of three steamers that once made regular trips through the Kissimmee valley:

> There is no more pleasant way of spending a week than to take the trip to Basinger. Birds of all kinds are in sight the whole way; flocks of ducks, coots, herons, cranes, limpkins, curlews, plume birds and water turkeys without end. Also alligators, rabbits and water snakes and plenty of fish, too. In its narrowness, in the rampant growth of water plants along its low banks, in the unbroken flatness of the landscape, in the labyrinth of by-channels and cut-offs and above all in the appalling, incredible, bewilder-

ing crookedness of its serpentine body, it is indeed an extraordinary river.

The Kissimmee could be confusing to navigate, especially when its wide floodplain was inundated with water. In 1882, Archie P. Williams and his expedition found themselves sailing on a flooded Kissimmee. Despair was setting in as light faded. "We look in vain for some friendly clump of trees in the distance, under which we may pitch our tents for the night," he wrote. "Nothing meets the eyes but sky, marsh and water, without a foot of dry land in sight."

Bubba Mills, working as a cattleman in the mid-twentieth century, became accustomed to the frequent flooding of the river. And he understood the ecological benefits, as he revealed in this essay in the Friends of the Everglades newsletter in 1982:

Fig. 30. Julia Thompson and Bob Mindick paddle Lake Kissimmee during a rare calm period.

Once a year we would join our neighbors and gather our stray cattle which had crossed the river to Duck Slough or had stopped mid-way on the grassy islands within the river. The cattle would be fat and the calves were always real good. We swam our horses from island to island until all cattle were retrieved and driven back home. We looked forward to this great venture each year.

The river, swollen by summer rains, would flood the original valley and then take the excess waters to Lake Okeechobee for storage and use during the dry months. The sheet flow of water brought new life to the valley by destroying the unwanted vegetation and restoring fresh grasses and new growth for the coming winter. This was nature's way for providing a suitable place for birds, wildlife, and even man, to thrive.

Fig. 31. Aerial view of the restored middle section of the Kissimmee River with a remnant of the former canal visible. Photo by Brent Anderson, South Florida Water Management District.

Fig. 32. A great egret. Bird life was abundant along the Kissimmee chain of lakes and restored Kissimmee River. Photo by Bob Mindick.

Fig. 33. A white ibis. Photo by Bob Mindick.

Long-term flooding made the Kissimmee unique among most North American rivers. Sometimes the floodplain was inundated for twelve consecutive months, or longer. "Flooding was the driver behind the Kissimmee's high biological productivity," said Joe Koebel, senior environmental scientist for the South Florida Water Management District. "Long-term inundation of the floodplain provided aquatic invertebrates, fishes, and other wildlife with excellent habitat for feeding, growing, and reproducing. These food resources were then available to larger predators such as largemouth bass, wading birds, waterfowl, and numerous birds of prey. Not only was the floodplain highly productive, but continuous flow in the river channel maintained relatively high levels of dissolved oxygen and high-quality habitat that created near-perfect conditions for aquatic invertebrates—the base of the food chain."

Aquatic invertebrates include such creatures as insects, mollusks, worms, crayfish, and freshwater shrimp. According to Koebel, nearly every creature in the river system feeds on aquatic invertebrates at some point in its life span. Translation: amphibians, reptiles, birds, fish, and some mammals found suitable habitat and abundant food in the Kissimmee River and floodplain.

Birds were a prime ecological indicator, and the Kissimmee was renowned for them. Archie Williams describes the bird life while floating the river at night in 1882:

> We have struck a rookery of water-fowl, and the water ahead is a moving mass of the feathered tribe, flapping their wings and beating the water, without giving forth a single sound from their throats. They do not attempt to fly until our boats are among them, and then it seems as if pandemonium had broken loose. As they rise they strike against the boatsmen's oars, and the mast of our boat, and we actually feel the touch of their wings as they bring their upward flight toward the banks, and then light among the reed and cane, to resume their perches in the water after we pass. By the light which streams across the river from our bow we are able to discern a dozen different varieties of the crane specie. The common white and blue cranes, the egrets with their long beautiful white plumes, flamingoes, curlews, and the water turkey, are among the varieties we note in their hurried flight.

But the same flooding that brought biological prosperity and beauty to the river led to its demise. After World War II, larger numbers of people moved into the Kissimmee basin. When growing towns such as Kissimmee became flooded for weeks after large storms, the Kissimmee River was blamed since water flowed so slowly through its wide floodplain, backing up water in the chain of lakes.

Enter the United States Army Corps of Engineers. From 1962 through 1971, the Army Corps of Engineers cut a straight ditch through the river's heart—reducing its length by half—to speed the flow of water to Lake Okeechobee. More than 35,000 acres of wetlands dried up. As a result, fish, waterfowl, and other wildlife drastically declined. Water was no longer being filtered by a slow meandering river channel through its expansive marshlands—kidneys for any natural system. Lake Okeechobee received too much water too quickly during the rainy season, forcing the South Florida Water Management District to dump excess water through canals to the Gulf of Mexico and to the Atlantic Ocean. And because the water quality was often severely degraded, Lake Okeechobee and estuaries on both coasts began to suffer from harmful algae blooms.

Meanwhile, because of the Kissimmee canalization and other major changes in the system, the Everglades below the big lake did not receive the normal amount of water during the dry season, and the entire system was thrown off-kilter. Fish and wildlife suffered in this biological domino effect. Even the upper chain of lakes was affected since water was no longer being backed up in the system by a slow-moving river. Boaters complained they were running aground in some of the lakes—formerly a rare occurrence.

In 1981, ten years after the last floating suction dredges and draglines had left the Kissimmee River, I was assigned to write an article about the damaged waterway for the short-lived *Geojourney* magazine; I felt as if I had stepped into a cloud of angry yellow jackets. I talked with environmental activists, land managers, and ranchers, who were all deadlocked in their disagreement over the river's fate. Should it somehow be restored, or should the impacts simply be accepted as part of civilization's "march of progress"?

One champion of restoration was Johnny Jones of the Florida Wildlife Federation. "When I was a teenage boy, we used to go over on the Kissimmee and go fishing and do a little duck hunting and things like that," he said in 1981. "It was just a place that I fell in love with and everybody who ever used the area fell in love with it; it just was a unique place. And it's a very beautiful river that's just been destroyed."

Chief beneficiaries of the Kissimmee's canalization were the owners of now dry marsh and floodplain. Improved pastureland in the valley increased by nearly 15,000 acres. Unimproved pastureland made similar expansions. "There's no way man can put it back like it was," Pat Wilson of the Latt Maxcy cattle and citrus corporation told me at the time. The company owned more than thirteen miles of riverfront. "Whether the project was right or wrong, it's there. Throwing good money after bad just doesn't make sense." Before, during, and after canalization, most of Wilson's land in the Kissimmee floodplain remained in native marshland, fodder for his cattle. Dechannelization, he said, would flood his land as it did historically, providing free fertilizer but also restricting grazing during certain seasons.

Richard Coleman of the Sierra Club and Kissimmee Restoration Coalition sounded a defiant tone: "We're going to do it one way or another [dechannelization]. And if man doesn't do it, God will—when we can't afford the energy and materials to maintain the ditch." The diverse environmental coalition was made up of conservation groups, garden clubs, the Winter Haven Chamber of Commerce, and the Central Florida Power Boat Association.

Marjory Stoneman Douglas, the Everglades' most famous and eloquent spokesperson, was in the thick of the Kissimmee battles. Her 1947 The Everglades: River of Grass in 1947 became the work against which all other Everglades books are measured, but in her later years she became much more than a writer. She personified the term "environmental activist."

When I lobbied for environmental causes in the late 1970s and early 1980s, I often observed Douglas testifying at Florida government hearings in Tallahassee. She was more than ninety years old then and still sharp. Her words were eloquent, her voice sometimes scolding, and she wouldn't compromise her goal of restoring the entire Everglades system.

Douglas had teamed up with the noted scientist Arthur R. Marshall, who took five minutes just to list his credentials. Between the two of them, they straightforwardly outlined a century of environmental abuse. They described how vast areas of Everglades had been converted to urban areas and farms; how levees and canals cut off vital sheet flow; how water often flowed at the wrong time and in insufficient or excess quantities; and how pollutants from agricultural runoff had taken a toll on wildlife populations. Moreover, they bemoaned the loss of the Kissimmee River, how a natural winding waterway had been converted into a 52-mile pollution-filled ditch, draining more and more water off of the historic floodplains. "Wasteful and stupid beyond words," summarized Douglas, never one to mince words.

Marshall often lectured on Everglades weather patterns. Evapotranspiration was integral to the entire system, I once heard him explain to a nonscientific Senate panel. Evaporation from Lake Okeechobee and the shallow, slow-moving river of grass below it often formed clouds that, in turn, would drift north and drop rain above Lake Okeechobee in the Kissimmee chain of lakes and Kissimmee River and other streams, and feed the system again. A rain machine, some have called it—an age-old cycle.

Marshall wrote about the process in 1982 for the Friends of the Everglades:

> Management of water in the Everglades, as established over many decades, has converted it from the solar driven system it was to a highly intensive fossil-fuel system. This exchange drastically displaces the solar-driven processes which produce wetland vegetation, peat and muck, potable water, fish and wildlife. The prime means through which solar energy activated the system to produce those essential resources was sheet flow—an essential function which has largely been lost. It is only necessary to reestablish sheet flow to regain solar energy products from the Everglades.

Engineers, however, are nervous about depending upon historic weather patterns. It can't always be measured, and it may vary from year to year. Plus, there is not complete agreement among the scientific community over how much rain is generated by the Everglades and how much blows in from the Atlantic.

Douglas and Marshall, along with other activists, testified at countless legislative hearings about the Kissimmee River, but they were far from satisfied with the results. "As far as we got was a resolution from the Florida House of Representatives telling a U.S. Senate Committee to tell the Army Corps of Engineers to tell its employees to study the possibility of breaking down the Kissimmee Canal, so the river could meander again," Douglas said in her 1987 autobiography, written with John Rothchild. "Congress voted $60,000 for the engineers to study this. Of course, they love to study it. They'd keep on studying it until the cows came home. Then they'd ask for more money for another study."

For Douglas, Marshall, and many others, the vision of restoring the Kissimmee never dimmed, however. "The river is still there," Marshall wrote to Douglas to buoy her spirits. "It's the water that's been taken away. The river is still there."

The Everglades and Kissimmee River eventually became everyone's sweetheart, and few politicians publicly opposed restoration. "The economy of government planning is obvious," said Reubin Askew, Florida governor from 1971 to 1979, "when you consider that it might have kept us from spending $50 million ruining the Kissimmee River in the name of flood control."

When Bob Graham took over the governorship in 1979, he dragged his feet on Kissimmee restoration while trying to elicit support for other priorities from an uncooperative legislature. The exact date of Graham's wake-up call regarding the Kissimmee was February 9, 1981. That's when *Sports Illustrated* published their popular swimsuit edition featuring Christie Brinkley and other sun-baked models. On page 82, in stark contrast to the bikini-clad women, a headline superimposed on the C-38 Canal proclaimed, "There's Trouble in Paradise." The scathing article about Florida's downward environmental spiral featured the ruined Kissimmee River front and center. Johnny Jones boldly griped that while Graham was environmentally friendly as a legislator, the green brush had not been carried over to the governor's office. "As a governor, he ain't got it," Jones summarized.

Since I was walking the halls of the Capitol at the time, I remember the reverberations caused by the article. For a high-profile politician like Graham to bear the brunt of public criticism in a national magazine was a public relations nightmare. Everyone wondered how he would react. Would he swear off Johnny Jones and other conservationists forever, or would he start being proactive as the state's highest elected official? Graham called Jones into a meeting, and it wasn't to give him a tongue-lashing. He sought to listen. And Jones, the former plumber, was smart enough to bring along Arthur Marshall. After an hour of hearing about the homes being built in the Kissimmee basin and that it was now or never, and of hearing Marshall outline his "Marshall Plan" for the Everglades system, Graham promised to act.

Bob Graham's bold Save Our Everglades program placed restoring the Kissimmee River at the top of the list. "We face an awesome truth," Graham said in unveiling the plan. "Our presence here is as tenuous as that of the fragile Everglades. . . . Whatever the price, the price of inaction is higher still."

Ranchers and homeowners along the river quickly formed a group called ROAR, Residents Organized Against Restoration. They had two pit bulls on their side. One was the Army Corps of Engineers, which claimed that, legally, it needed economic justification—in clear dollars and cents—to restore the river; their agency wasn't mandated to work on pure environmental projects. Their other ally was the Reagan administration. The federal government was backing away from using public money to buy environmental lands, and for the Kissimmee restoration to succeed, the floodplains would have to be purchased.

It was only after Graham left the governorship to become a United States senator that he succeeded in making real progress for the Kissimmee. In 1990, he inserted language into a public works bill that authorized the Corps to take on purely environmental projects. Two years later, Congress directed the Corps to restore the Kissimmee River, and environmental projects now take up about a fifth of the Corps' workload.

While studying the issue, the Corps had considered several alternatives, ranging from complete backfilling of the canal to simply plugging the canal at key locations. The option finally chosen was a compromise—backfill part of the canal, remove two of the five dams, and restore the middle section of the old Kissimmee River channel and floodplain. Control structures would remain at the top and bottom of the river and between the chain of lakes to control flooding.

Coming up with a plan was one thing, however; carrying it out was quite another. The burden of buying the expansive Kissimmee floodplain fell primarily to the South Florida Water Management District, and purchasing land from ranchers who had long fought restoration was no easy task. It took several years, professional mediators, and tens of millions of dollars to purchase enough land for phase one of the project.

Fig. 34. Spoil areas from the huge canal dug through the heart of the Kissimmee River.

Finally, in 1999, environmental history turned a new page. Engineers along the Kissimmee were once again turning dirt, this time to help remediate past wrongs. More than seven miles of the C-38 Canal were backfilled, water was diverted into the old river channel, and long-dormant wetlands began coming back to life.

A key dam on the river was blown up. Sequential photographs of the destruction were featured on the Army Corps of Engineers Web site with apparent pride. Blow up a dam for conservation? It was enough to make any battle-scarred environmentalist flush with pride. I can picture Art Marshall, Marjory Stoneman Douglas, and other Kissimmee activists who have gone to the great river beyond perched atop a cypress tree to view the explosion, with the ever-optimistic Marshall commenting, "Well, Marjory, I knew we could do it." And the feisty Douglas responding, scrunching up her nose, "It's about damn time!"

In 2006, another milestone was reached: Florida had acquired enough land along the chain of lakes and Kissimmee River to complete the restoration. In all, 43 miles of winding river and 28,800 acres of wetlands will be restored, and another dam will meet a glorious end. At a cost of more than a half billion dollars, it is considered the largest true ecosystem restoration project in the world, and it has attracted ecologists from throughout the world who seek to resurrect their damaged rivers.

But the Kissimmee above the restoration area is still a woeful ghost of its former self. On our trip, we poked into the old river channels along the C-38 Canal and had difficulty paddling any distance. Starved of water, these oxbows were mostly shallow and weed-choked, while the canal was wide, deep, and arrow-straight, the water largely depleted of life-supporting oxygen. As far as fish were concerned, mostly gar and bowfin tolerated these waters.

Stopping for a rest, we climbed tall, angular spoil berms of sand and muck created by the canal dredging. These effigy mounds from an engineer's dreamworld stretched across vast areas of former wetlands. Scanning the massive creations, I wondered how our species evolved to have such divergent visions regarding the environment. One group seeks to create order through efficient canals and locks and dams, while another prefers the pulse of natural systems. I yearned to see firsthand, in the days to come, how these two dreamworlds had merged to resurrect part of the Kissimmee River.

chapter 8

~~~~~~~~~~~~~~~~~~~~

Trail Dreams

Paddling that afternoon in the canal was a bit monotonous. I hummed songs, talked with my mates, called friends on my cell phone, and watched for gators. "This is the true alligator alley," observed Bob. "It must have been a spectacular place to have explored pre-channelization." He counted thirty-five gators by day's end. Unfortunately for Bob, he had to leave that evening, replaced by his pleasant coworker Julia.

At the end of the day, we paddled a half mile on the old river channel to our campsite at the Kicco (pronounced Kiss-oh) town site, an early cattle town that was part of the Kissimmee Island Cattle Company. At one time, this cattle-drive staging area boasted homes, a mess hall, bunkhouse, store, icehouse, power plant, schoolhouse, and steamboat landing. When cattle drives became a thing of the past, so did the town. Nothing remains of Kicco today except for some concrete foundations and sidewalks and an open area the size of a football field. A handful of live oaks shade picnic tables and a spacious camping area used by Florida Trail hikers who have followed an old cattle-droving trail for several miles.

The ambitious Florida Trail is a 1,400-mile footpath extending from Big Cypress Swamp to the far reaches of the Florida Panhandle, the dream of the real estate broker and wildlife photographer Jim Kern. I was able to speak with Kern about the trail in 2003. The idea, he said, came to him in the early 1960s after he made a short but disastrous hike on the Appalachian Trail. "When I got back to Miami, I wondered about where you can go hiking in Florida," said Kern, who now resides in St. Augustine. "There weren't many places. I realized right away that there should be a footpath the length of Florida, through the wildest parts of the state—through the Ocala, Osceola, and Apalachicola national forests, along the banks of the Suwannee River, and I looked for other scenic spots and public land. It came together pretty quickly in my mind."

Kern found others of like mind and formed the nonprofit Florida Trail Association (FTA) in 1964. Volunteer chapters sprang up around the state, and trail blazing began in earnest on both public and private lands.

But there were formidable obstacles. Agreements with private landowners were often on a handshake basis; they could be changed on a whim, and some landowners simply refused passage. Over time, it became apparent that major gaps in the trail would be difficult to bridge without outside help. And so the trail received a boost in 1983, when Congress designated the Florida Trail a national scenic trail. The USDA Forest Service was charged with developing a comprehensive plan for the trail, and money was eventually appropriated for hiring staff and buying trail corridors.

While traditional FTA partners included the Forest Service and several state agencies, the FTA is now working with more nontraditional partners, such as paper companies and the United States Air Force. More than fifty miles of new trail were constructed through the Eglin Air Force Base in the Panhandle. Along the Kissimmee River just below Kicco Camp, more than twenty miles of trail ran through the Avon Park Bombing Range. Fortunately, our hiking team members received permission to walk through in the morning since the air force rarely bombs on a Friday.

Nearly three-quarters of the entire trail is officially certified as part of the Florida National Scenic Trail, meaning that these sections meet minimum guidelines for access, trail management, and a protected trail corridor. "I can't help but be pleased by what's been accomplished," said Jim Kern. "The Florida Trail Association has a reputation as a sharp, can-do organization." Kern says that he feels awkward about receiving praise for his early role in the FTA. "So many people put in volunteer time working on the trail. Last year, volunteers put in sixty thousand hours. That is remarkable."

The Florida Trail is unique when compared to other national scenic trails such as the Appalachian Trail in that long-distance hikers have alternative routes to choose from. They can hike along the east or west side of the Lake Okeechobee dike, and they can take an east or west route around Orlando and a big chunk of central Florida. Trail planners believe the central Florida loop is a good way of utilizing existing trails, such as the Cross Florida Greenway and footpaths through the Withlacoochee State Forest. Plus, it better serves population centers in Tampa and Orlando.

"The trail connects the disparate parts of the Sunshine State together," concludes Johnny Molloy, a 2007 Florida Trail thru-hiker, in his *Hiking the Florida Trail*, "and walking the trail is a way to make sense of Florida's far flung divisions."

Despite its successes, remaining gaps in the Florida Trail require thru-hikers (those attempting to walk the entire distance) to walk highways, back roads, and logging roads. About 300 to 400 more miles must be acquired to take the trail completely off of roads. Fortunately, in one of the trail's most remote sections—along the Kissimmee River—much of the trail corridor has been purchased by the water management district.

Most thru-hikers tend to hike the trail from south to north, beginning in midwinter, so for northbound hikers, the last town before the Kissimmee River segment is Okeechobee. As in many trail towns, hikers can do their laundry, check in a motel, take a shower, and go to the post office. And in Okeechobee, they can call on one of many "trail angels" along the way—Doug and Pat McCoy. "We have two kids, so we can't get out as much as we'd like," said Doug McCoy, a middle school teacher in Okeechobee. "So, we enjoy helping thru-hikers. They can shower, stay a night or two, and we can shuttle them to places. We have a swimming pool, lots of space, a pool table, so it's very relaxing for them. There's not a lot of civilization for 150 miles or so north of here, so Okeechobee is a good place to stop."

Among the interesting people who have stayed with the McCoys is Eb Eberhart, otherwise known as the Nimblewill Nomad. He hiked from Key West to Canada, and then back down to Key West. Afterward, he started heading west across the United States.

In 2001, the six-member "Hike for Hope" group stayed with the McCoys. They were making a 4,440-mile trek from Florida to Canada for Oxfam America, an antihunger group.

Thru-hikers spread the news about trail angels to other hikers via word of mouth and logbook entries, and more and more thru-hikers are hiking the Florida Trail every year. Many thru-hikers use the Florida Trail as the first leg of a longer journey. Some begin their trek in Key West, well below the southern terminus of the Florida Trail, and after three or so months of hiking the Florida Trail, they head north through the Florida Panhandle's Blackwater State Forest and on into southern Alabama. From there, they connect with a series of trails that lead to the 2,150-mile Appalachian Trail. Once they reach Mount Katahdin, Maine, after another five or six months of hiking, they hike the International Appalachian Trail to Canada and eventually end their trek at the Gulf of St. Lawrence in Quebec, where the Appalachian Mountains dramatically end at the Cliffs of Forillon.

All trails, and all long treks, start with a dream. Fred Davis, director of the land stewardship division for the water management district, had a couple of trail dreams. He had joined the hiking contingent of our group that day, a group including Mike, Beth, Ian, and a new member, Doug Hattaway of the Trust for Public Land, who switched off with Dale Allen. Fred had long envisioned a paddling trail through the Kissimmee valley, and for it to be developed similar to the 170-mile Suwannee River Wilderness Trail. On that high-profile north Florida trail, paddlers have the option of primitive camping or staying in either screened pavilions or cabins at ten- to fifteen-mile intervals along much of the river.

With retirement only a month away, and after thirty-five years of public service, Fred planned to hoist a backpack for the entire length of the Appalachian Trail. What better way to begin a new stage of life? "I'm doing it because I want to," said Fred, "not because I have to prove anything. If it stops being fun, I'm coming home. I'm just glad my wife is allowing me to go for six months because I'd rather do a thru-hike than a series of section hikes."

I hiked the mountainous 2,000-plus-mile trail just out of high school and have pondered hiking it again when I retire, or maybe I'll tackle the Florida Trail. There's something about long treks that can be particularly helpful during major transition periods in life. They are rites of passage. Those hours, days, weeks, and months of exercise and fresh air help one to think and focus on what's really important.

In that vein, Expedition Headwaters was proving important for me in that I would reach the half-century mark in only a few days, on April 4. During my packing for the expedition, I had included several items that I rarely needed on the Appalachian Trail at age eighteen, however. They were mostly painkillers, salves, and omega 3 oils for joint pains and muscle aches. As it turned out, I needed very little of it. In terms of soreness, I felt better than before I left, mainly because I wasn't sitting at a desk for hours on end—the worst punishment for a body. But the trip wasn't over, and perhaps the most challenging day would begin at sunrise. Both the hikers and paddlers would have to travel more than twenty miles under their own power, enough to challenge anyone. As added bonuses, the paddlers would have to traverse the current river restoration project—a two-mile-long construction site—followed by a long bushwhack through the river floodplain to the planned campsite. The expedition had certainly gotten interesting.

chapter 9

~~~~~~~

Restoration!

Disaster struck in the morning. "Flesh-eating" red ants had invaded my kayak during the night, and it was a complete infestation. I had to flood the cockpit several times before it was safe to sit. The water around the launch swirled with biting, angry ants.

Virginia, on the other hand, was having her own challenges. Being an anchorwoman, appearance was everything, but dolling up for the camera could be difficult while primitive camping. Determined to wash her hair in something other than river water, she collected all of the half-empty water bottles in camp along with water from the bottom of an ice chest and took a freezing shower. Then she started the film crew's generator to blow-dry her hair and used her editing table and a vehicle mirror to apply makeup. Life in the bush is rough for television personalities.

Once ready to embark, Julia and I started paddling toward the C-38 Canal on part of the old river channel, enjoying the quiet beauty. Bream popped and little blue herons poked along the shallows—an idyllic Florida scene. Suddenly, we heard a loud mechanical whop, whop, whop above us, like a hovering airboat. On the first day, the film crew had warned us about occasional helicopter visits. "Just act natural and keep paddling," Virginia had said. "And don't look up." They followed us for several minutes, and by the time they left, we were on the C-38 Canal, and the magic of the natural channel had faded. Future paddlers will likely miss out on such interruptions.

On the canal, the miles passed quickly as we chatted and hummed songs. Around lunch time, we waited for the hikers at a Florida Trail intersection on the live oak bluffs of Fort Kissimmee, once the site of a log fort hastily built in 1837 during the Second Seminole War. Skirmishes between Colonel Zachary Taylor's roughly one thousand troops and bands of Seminoles around Lake Tohopekaliga near the present-day Kissimmee airport had prompted Taylor to march south and build several forts within a day's march of each other—Fort Gardner between lakes Hatchineha and Kissimmee, Fort Kissimmee, and Fort Bassinger, about fifteen miles above Lake Okeechobee along the river. Taylor confronted small bands of war-weary Seminoles along the way, and several surrendered, including the Seminole leader Jumper and sixty-three of his followers.

All of this activity led up to one of the largest battles of the war. Hot on the trail of a large band of Seminoles, Taylor veered southeast from the Kissimmee River toward Lake Okeechobee. John K. Mahon, in his classic *History of the Second Seminole War 1835–1842*, describes what happened next, on Christmas Day:

> By moving at daylight, the army entered one large camp in which the fires were still burning, although the Indians had fled. Then, they captured a single warrior in an open prairie (probably planted there) who showed them where the foe was settled into position ready to fight.
>
> Never had Indians prepared a battleground with greater care. They were in a hammock with about half a mile of swamp in front of them, and Lake Okeechobee not far to their rear. The sawgrass in the swamp stood five feet high, and mud and water were three feet deep. The Seminoles had cut down the grass to provide a corridor for fire, and had notched the trees in their hammock to steady their guns. Believing themselves virtually impregnable, from 380 to 480 Indians waited attack. Old Sam Jones, although not a war chief, commanded more than half of them on the right, Alligator led 120 in the center, and Coacoochee, crazy for revenge, held the left with about 80 followers. Seminoles and others were segregated, as usual, into separate groups. As a result, they were not a cohesive fighting force sub-

ject to the direction of one unifying will. And it was their misfortune that the largest body of Negro warriors was not present.

Taylor, overcoming the advice of one commander who wanted to encircle their foes and attack from different flanks, ordered a direct assault. As a result, most of the advance units were cut down, either killed or wounded. The Seminoles made it a habit of aiming for officers, and this strategy proved effective. Mahon writes:

> the heaviest fire bored into five companies of the Sixth in the corridor cut through the sawgrass. When all but one of their company officers and most of the noncoms had been hit, these five companies retired and reformed. At this moment Colonel Ramsey Thompson of the Sixth was fatally hit. Propped against a tree facing the foe, he called out "Remember the regiment to which you belong!" and so died. Once the frontal attack was strongly pressed, Taylor ordered the First Infantry, the reserve, to reach the enemy's right and hit him in that flank. As soon as the First got into position, the Indians gave one final volley and began to retreat. . . . The Indians withdrew toward the lake, scattered, and escaped toward the east.

> Even though outnumbered two to one, the Seminoles elected to stand and fight at Okeechobee only because they thought they could inflict more harm than they would receive. The casualties indicated that their estimate was right; the white force lost 26 killed and 112 wounded, compared to the Seminoles' 11 and 14. The fight was over by three o'clock. There was no pursuit because Taylor had so many dead and wounded to evacuate.

Despite the lopsided toll of casualties, Taylor claimed victory because the Seminoles had retreated. Heroic descriptions of the battle were released to the public, Taylor soon became a brigadier general, and his stature on the political horizon was greatly enhanced. After successes in the Mexican War, Taylor rode his fame to the White House, becoming the twelfth president of the United States.

For the Seminoles, most were killed or removed to the Oklahoma Territory. A handful successfully evaded pursuit in the Everglades until the Third Seminole War erupted in 1857, when a surveying party started destroying the garden of Chief Billy Bowlegs II. During the ensuing conflict, thirty Seminoles were captured along the Lower Kissimmee River, and Bowlegs and his band of 134 Seminoles, hounded by troops, surrendered in 1858. They were boarded onto a steamer for the sad journey west and stopped to resupply at St. Marks, along Florida's Big Bend Gulf coast. It was here that Polly Parker, also known as Ma-de-lo-yee, escaped and walked more than three hundred miles back to the Kissimmee River country.

The late Seminole storyteller Mary Johns used to tell of a group of Seminole people who got tired of running and fighting during the Seminole wars and simply became invisible. They still live on an island in the Kissimmee River, she had said.

The Florida Seminoles who escaped the third prolonged attempt at removal persisted as a cohesive tribe. When the United States became gripped in the throes of Civil War, various Seminoles such as Chief Chipco and his band felt safe enough to move out of the Big Cypress Swamp and return to their traditional hunting grounds in the Kissimmee River region. The Third Seminole War had not destroyed the friendships established with select settlers, and they lived in relative peace. Today, the Florida Seminoles number in the thousands and have reservations from Tampa to Hollywood. Brighton Reservation, located west of the Kissimmee River on the northwest shore of Lake Okeechobee, is one of the largest.

In the past half century, the Seminole Tribe has become a trendsetter. They were the first North American tribe to venture into the gambling business in 1979, and the first to buy a large international corporation when they purchased the Hard Rock business—including casinos, cafes, hotels, and concert venues—for nearly $1 billion in 2006. The tribe is now owner of the world's largest collection of rock ' n' roll memorabilia.

Imagine a Seminole shaman decades before—maybe around a fire surrounded by traditional open-sided palm-thatched *chickees* and along a swampy shore lined with dugout canoes—announcing to his startled clansmen that someday the tribe would own successful business establishments in the world's largest cities and be the primary keepers of historical items pertaining to the world's most popular music with a tribal beat. That the Seminoles have moved from being the hunted to being financial players on the world stage boggles the mind. At a New York news conference to announce the deal, the tribal vice chairman Max Osceola quipped, "We're going to buy Manhattan back one hamburger at a time."

Beth was the first of the hikers to arrive at the Fort Kissimmee bluffs. A former sprinter in college, she had strong legs and a fast pace. Being the lead hiker had its advantages and disadvantages. There were spider webs to clear, but also wildlife to observe. "I had deer run about me being playful and seeming to show me the way," she said.

Beth's most heart-pounding episode that morning, however, didn't involve an animal, but a person. She was climbing a stile to enter the cathedral-like live oak and palm trail section through the Avon Park Bombing Range when she noticed a movement out of the corner of her eye. "I looked to my left, and there was this guy in full camo with a rifle in hand slinking out from behind a tree," she said. "I froze and stood motionless, but after a moment I figured that if he planned to shoot, I'd be dead already, so on with the hike I went. I'm glad I was wearing orange!" The official Florida Trail hats and T-shirts are a bright "hunter orange" for a reason.

When Doug Hattaway walked up a half hour later, he said he had run into the same hunter. "He was hunting turkeys," he said to Beth, "and he said that as you stepped over the fence, you passed right through his line of sight on a turkey."

"No shit!" Beth exclaimed.

Ian and Fred came in next. "Where's Mike?" Julia asked, worry in her voice. She and Mike were sweethearts.

"He's coming, but his feet are bothering him," said Fred.

Julia quickly dialed Mike on her cell phone. "How's it going? Would you like to switch with me and kayak the rest of the way? We can both be hiyakers today." A "hiyaker" was Julia's term for someone who both hiked and paddled on the expedition.

Mike initially refused the offer, but when he finally straggled into the lunch spot, slightly limping, and with more than twelve miles to go, he relented. With his military background, I knew he didn't like to admit weakness, but there was no ranking officer barking orders out here, no forced marches. All of the participants had the freedom to paddle, hike, or help transport supplies in a support vehicle being driven in this stretch by Deb Blick of the Florida Trail Association. She had relieved Ayounga Riddick.

Mike and I soon embarked from the bluff and I could tell he was relieved to be in a kayak. After a couple of miles, we approached a construction zone of the current Kissimmee River restoration project. Signs warned boaters to turn back, but we had advance permission to enter the area and were met by two officials with the Army Corps of Engineers wearing hardhats. They politely told us how to navigate through the area. "Up ahead, you'll see the channel on your right. Just take that," the more senior of the two told us. "That's where we had to recarve part of the old river channel that had been destroyed by the canal. There's some shallow spots, but you should be able to make it through." For the recarving project, the Corps consulted with biologists and used old maps of the original channel.

Mike and I paddled on. Huge yellow dump trucks rumbled past. They carried dirt from former spoil berms to an area of canal being filled, forcing water into the carved channel. Then we encountered

Fig. 35. A dump truck lumbers over a makeshift bridge, carrying fill from spoil areas to deposit in the canal that was cut through the river in the 1960s and early 1970s.

Fig. 36. A construction zone of the current restoration project. The restored Kissimmee River is to the right; the canal being filled is to the left.

floating yellow turbidity barriers that kept soil from drifting into the river, but they presented an obstacle for us. The banks were steep and muddy, discouraging us from portaging, and the barriers weren't stable enough to stand on to slide our boats across. After trial and error, the best method to move over them, we learned, was to paddle into the row of barriers at full throttle and shoot over the top.

As we wound around the construction site through the carved channel—admiring how the Corps had duplicated the natural bends and twists of a natural river (even engineers can get it right!)—several baby alligators about a forearm in size scurried along the bank. Then the eight-foot-long mother shot off an embankment, belly flopping into the river. "Whoa!" Mike cried. "I wasn't expecting that."

On the other side of the construction site, our two Corps friends were waiting on the shore to make sure we made it through. They waved and took photos. We were likely the first boaters to test their creation, although the alligators had obviously taken to it right away.

When we entered the historic river channel, its flow newly restored, a subtle feeling of jubilation came over me. The lifeblood of the river—

Fig. 37. We learned that the best method to move over the floating yellow turbidity barriers in the Kissimmee River restoration construction zone was to ram them at full speed and try to shoot over the top.

water—had returned after a long absence, seeming to awaken a sleeping beauty. Serpentine twists and bends through lush marshlands, occasionally bordered by sandy banks and cypress and live oak trees, added mystery and beauty. Meandering. Unpredictable. If ever there was a proper feng shui for paddlers, this was it. With no canal to divert flow, we finally felt we were on the Kissimmee River as it had been for eons.

For nearly thirty years, this channel had been virtually impassable, clogged by muck and aquatic weed growth such as water hyacinth and water lettuce, but the return of water flow flushed out the channel within six months. Long-buried sandbars reemerged. Dry-land trees that had encroached into the floodplain started dying back. Once-dormant native plants such as the pink-tipped smartweed, the jointed stems of horsetail, and various sedges and rushes popped up along the shores. Vast stretches of soggy broadleaf marsh began to thrive in what were once dry cow pastures, bahia grass replaced by leathery green arrowhead plants, white-flowered duck potato, and purple-topped pickerel weed. The native seeds had been embedded in the soil since before canalization, waiting for the water that would bring them to life.

As the reemerging wetlands began to filter excess nutrients from the water, the flushing of the channel and turbulent mixing from the restored flow led to a dramatic increase in dissolved oxygen levels in the river. The result was a biological boon. While scientists attest to a rapid rise in aquatic invertebrates in the river channel such as filtering caddis flies and larval midges that small fish thrive on, anglers rave about the improved fisheries. Catches of bass and bream are reminiscent of the old Kissimmee. Even fishing professionals are taking notice. The 2006 CITGO Bassmaster Classic second-place winner, Rick Morris, boated all the way down from Lake Toho to the restored section of the Kissimmee for his winning catches.

With all of the ecosystem improvements, animals at the top of the food chain are naturally benefiting. Mike and I started keeping track of the numerous alligators we encountered. By day's end, the total was in excess of 150. Many topped ten feet in length. Since becoming scarce as a result of illegal poaching, Florida's restrictions on the commercial trade of alligator skins have helped the alligator population to

Fig. 38. Alligators were abundant along the restored section of the Kissimmee River. Photo by Bob Mindick.

rebound. In the past, some Florida cattlemen are said to have waged war against alligator poachers because wet "gator holes" helped their livestock survive during drought periods.

Early accounts of alligators along the river and chain of lakes are the stuff of legend. Tourists on steamships and sailboats frequently shot at the reptiles for sport in much the same manner as railroad passengers blasted away at western bison from their window seats. Archie Williams, during the 1882 *New Orleans Times-Democrat* expedition, wrote:

> On all sides of us at times these huge monsters are to be seen floating on the water, or lying quietly on the banks sunning themselves. During the early morning we leave them unmolested, unless one is particularly bold, and use our shotguns among the ducks and jacksnipe; at about 11 or 12 o'clock shotguns are laid aside and with rifles we play havoc among the alligators. They are bold and fearless, and in several instances have been known to attack a single man. They are so seldom molested and shot that the crack of our rifles do not disturb them, unless a bullet takes effect, and then if not killed dead make things lively around them for awhile.

Few attempts were made to retrieve dead alligators for their hides or meat. One early dredge operator in the Southport Canal, as reported by Williams, complained that "it is not pleasant to have dead alligators floating down the canal and lodging against the dredge."

As early as 1873, writers such as Harriet Beecher Stowe, who settled along the St. Johns River, protested the wanton killing of alligators and other wildlife from Florida's pleasure boats. She writes in *Palmetto Leaves*:

> A parcel of hulking fellows sit on the deck of a boat, and pass through the sweetest paradise God ever made, without one idea of its loveliness, one gentle, sympathizing thought of the animal happiness with which the Creator has filled these recesses. All the way along is a constant fusillade upon every living thing that shows itself on the bank. Now a bird is hit, and hangs, head

downward, with a broken wing; and a coarse laugh choruses the deed. Now an alligator is struck; and the applause is greater.

For the area's Seminoles, and some Crackers and river rats, alligator hides were their primary source of barter and income. The going rate at the end of the nineteenth century was twenty-five cents to $2.50 a hide, depending on the size. To see the carcasses of bloated alligators floating in the waterways—shot by carefree tourists aboard steamships—must have seemed a terrible waste to those living on the edge of survival. By 1900, most of the really big alligators were gone from easily accessible waters, requiring hide hunters to venture into more remote regions of the Everglades and other swamps.

For the true alligator hunter, it wasn't quite as easy as shooting them from the bow of a steamer. The famous gator hunter Jesse Otis Beall, interviewed in 1997 by Dana Ste. Claire, recalled swimming into an alligator hole and hooking a beast that was almost twelve feet long. "I had a rope tied to the pole and came back out and pulled him out," he said. "I wasn't scared of him and I think the alligators knew that. I just was not ascared of him. I could wade in a hole with one and not be feared, no fear a'tall and I think he was ascared of me more than I was of him." Today, only licensed hunters help to manage the populations.

Since the day was warm and we hadn't had a shower in three days, Mike and I decided to rinse off in the river. The problem was the alligators. They were around every bend, and as part of their survival instinct, they would swim to deeper water and submerge to conceal themselves when we approached. Young ones would often do so with a furious splash, but the really big ones would swim and submerge with unnerving slowness, showing little fear. So we found a sandy spot and took turns wading in the water and splashing off, while the other stood guard with a kayak paddle, ready to fend off any curious reptilian life forms. Alligators rarely attack people unless they've been fed by human hands, and we doubted there were enough people who frequented this remote river to worry about that, but still . . .

Someone once said that true adventures were the result of poor planning, or, I might add, being unnecessarily careless. Neither of us wanted to end up as candidates for a Darwin Award—usually given posthumously to the person who departed this world in such a stupid fashion that he or she (usually a "he") benefited the gene pool by making an early exit. I could picture it—an excerpt of my log would describe the multitude of alligators, and the next line would say something like, "And then they decided to go swimming!"

Birds, on the other hand, didn't elicit an internal yellow flag. We noticed more bird life along the restored river than we'd seen along the canals—limpkins, green herons, yellowlegs, stilts, cormorants, and many others. Since the restoration, biologists have observed eight species of shorebirds that have not been seen along the river in thirty years, and they have documented a momentous increase in waterfowl and wading bird numbers and diversity. The Kissimmee, at least in this middle section, was back!

Fig. 39. A pair of black-necked stilts along the restored section of the Kissimmee River. These birds disappeared from the river in the early 1970s after the river was channelized, returning around 2002, after the first restoration phase was complete.

Fig.40. Close-up of a limpkin, one of the bird species that returned after part of the Kissimmee River was restored.

In all of our excitement in paddling the restored river, however, there was a worry. It was getting late, and the river wound unceasingly in tight curves. As the crow flies, my GPS showed our final destination for the evening to be only three miles at one point, but the distance would slightly increase and then decrease, and go back and forth for a spell as we navigated the hairpin curves of the channel. One newspaper reporter in 1899, as reported by Jim Robison in *Kissimmee: Gateway to the Kissimmee Valley*, bemoaned the Kissimmee's curves: "There are bends where it takes nearly an hours [*sic*] steaming to reach a spot less than a hundred yards ahead of the bow."

As the sun dipped lower, fatigue started setting in. "Aren't you glad you chose to paddle this afternoon?" I joked with Mike.

"We just seemed to wind and wind and never get anywhere," he observed. "But my feet feel fine!"

A kayak or small boat is the perfect craft for navigating the twisting bends of the old river, but historically, larger boats have tried—with extreme difficulty. The first and only large paddle wheeler to navigate the Kissimmee was the *Bertha Lee* in 1883. Purchased in the Ohio River valley by a Kissimmee hotel manager, the idea was to transport the influx of tourists around Lake Tohopekaliga on moonlight excursions and on guided trips to the islands. But first, the 130-foot-long steamer with the four- foot draft had to make it up the Kissimmee River. Edward A. Mueller describes the challenge in his 1966 *Tequesta* article "Kissimmee Steamboating":

In those days, the river was a snake's dream of heaven, being a crooked combination of narrow channels, sharp bends, cut-offs, dead rivers, and zig-zags in confounding numbers. Anything larger than a rowboat had pretty tough going.

The Bertha Lee finally got to Kissimmee City but not without literally cutting her own way at times across some of the sharper bends and using her paddlewheel to generate enough current to cause a scouring action and thus clear a short channel. Usually the steamboat would turn around, reversing direction and use her stern wheel to help clear the way, the process being known as fanning. After fifteen heartbreaking toilsome days of beating up the Kissimmee, the Bertha Lee had to dispatch a rowboat to Kissimmee as supplies were very low, owing to the extreme length of the extraordinary voyage. After a week they returned with provisions just as the crew were on their uppers. The Bertha Lee finally emerged triumphant at Kissimmee after a month and a half of very arduous voyaging from Ft. Myers. This undoubtedly was the most severe trip for any vessel on the Kissimmee River.

Unfortunately, for the owners, the big paddle wheeler did not turn out to be the renowned success they had envisioned in the upper chain of lakes. Only a year later, the *Bertha Lee* had to navigate the Kissimmee River again on its way to Ft. Myers. The ship did duty on the Suwannee and then hauled cotton on the Apalachicola and Chattahoochee rivers before it wrecked and capsized on a tight curve near Bristol, Georgia, soon after an expensive overhaul.

The Kissimmee today is actually quieter than in the era of the *Bertha Lee*. Highways have replaced the interior waterways as major thoroughfares for transportation, and one rarely sees a craft larger than a pontoon boat.

When Mike and I finally reached the mouth of a tiny creek that the map said was our spot to park our kayaks on shore—resting weary arms—we had a dilemma. Our predesignated campsite along the Florida Trail was more than a half mile away across the Kissimmee's wide floodplain. We could see the line of live oaks in the distance to the west; our GPS pointed to a slight dip in the treeline that marked our destination. The plan—largely devised in an office—was to traverse the floodplain on foot. So we took a deep breath and started wading waist-deep in marsh, water, and mud, not being able to see below our knees. The mud sucked off a shoe more than once. Mike and I glanced at each other. We didn't need to say aloud our biggest worry—snakes. If alligators were active on such a warm day, what about water moccasins? And we would have to wade back to the kayaks through this same floodplain in the morning. I paused and pulled out the map. Mike didn't need any encouragement to stop alongside and study it as well. "Look here," I said, pointing to a spot. "If we paddle down the river another half mile or so, it looks like the Florida Trail comes closer to the river. Maybe we can park the boats and hike on a dry trail to the campsite rather than wade through this."

"Let's do it," Mike agreed. Visually, we could see the line of trees merge closer to the river to the south. We assumed the Florida Trail followed this higher ground. Even with modern equipment such as GPS systems, it pays to know how to read a map and use visual clues from the terrain.

Mike's cell phone rang—another relatively modern invention that wasn't available to earlier expeditions. Mike had to turn his body to get a better signal. "I can barely hear you," he said. It was Julia. The hikers had arrived in camp and were worried about us since the paddlers had generally moved faster than the hikers for the past few days. Mike told her of our plan, and she planned to meet us with a big flashlight. Darkness was closing in.

Old spooky stories of this stretch of the Kissimmee below the Avon Park Bombing Range—one of the remotest regions in Florida—did flash through my mind as we pushed off again in our kayaks and paddled south down the shadowy stream. Alma Hetherington writes in *The River of the Long Water*:

> At a place in the river not far north from the Basinger landing and not too far from Alligator Bluff, strange noises were often heard. The water whirled in an agitated manner; and the bellow, which seemed to come from the depths of the river, could only be explained as perhaps the groans of a manatee caught in a log or the murmuring of wind through an underground passage.

Other blood-curdling tales include those of ghost pirates who are still fighting over buried treasure and the restless spirit of a man killed by an alligator, but none equals the one told by longtime boating enthusiast Rick Selzer. According to Selzer, as recorded by Dan Asfar in *Ghost Stories of Florida*, he was in his boat looking for a place to camp along the river when he heard loud splashes in a small bay bordered by thick growth along the main channel. He edged over to investigate. Instantly, he felt uneasy. "[I]t felt like everything was wrong," he said, "the water, the bush, everything. The sun was just starting to go down, and it was starting to get dark, but wasn't nearly dark enough to explain the color of the water. This water, it was *black*—way too black to be natural. I remember looking at it and thinking, *what is going on?*"

He started backing up the boat when the center of the water rose up and came down in a tremendous upheaval, followed by a massive churning. "Nothing that lives in the wetlands is big enough to make that kind of stir," he said. "But beyond its size, I could tell there was nothing there—there was nothing under the surface. The water was churning on its own, as if the whole bay was alive."

Rick quickly moved downriver and eventually found a place to camp. After setting up his tent and gear, eating dinner, and falling into a fitful sleep, an awful moan drew his attention again to the river. "I jumped out of my sleeping bag right away," he said. "The thing was so loud, it couldn't have been more than thirty feet away. . . . I ran out to the river, knife in one hand, flashlight in the other, more buzzed than scared. My blood was rushing, but I was more eager to see what this creature looked like than fearful." He saw nothing, heard nothing. Disappointed, he returned to his campsite only to find all of his gear upended. "My campsite looked like a hurricane had passed through

Fig. 41. In this stretch, the restored Kissimmee River meanders through a marshy floodplain more than two miles wide. To the left, a group of expedition members hike a long boardwalk of the Florida Trail.

it," he said. "My tent was collapsed, my sleeping bag was inside out, and draped over a bush, all my bags were emptied, my gear scattered all over the place." But none of the food had been touched or was missing, and he found no tracks. Rick stayed awake the rest of the night, and at first light, he drove the boat directly to his truck, vowing never to return to the Kissimmee River.

Fortunately, after Mike and I paddled downriver a spell in the fading light, we found the Florida Trail just as we had hoped. It was marked by a tall footbridge over a side channel. A boardwalk traversed part of the floodplain since a nearby rancher had refused access to the uplands. Julia soon found us, a big smile on her face. We stashed our boats, and she guided us to the camp. Mike dubbed the afternoon's adventure "Lewis and Doug."

We had survived the longest and perhaps most rewarding day of the trip thus far. As we walked, we watched a group of black wild hogs feeding in the marsh as the setting sun cast orange hues across the wide Kissimmee River floodplain. Natural rivers can be much more challenging than canals, we concluded, but their beauty is unsurpassed.

chapter 10

Kissimmee Wanderings

Julia was back in her kayak, and she and I continued on the restored Kissimmee River. The floodplain widened even more to where the Kissimmee resembled a river through a prairie, its marshy floodplain at least two miles wide. We stopped along the shore to gaze across the expanse since a kayak makes for a poor vantage point when trying to see above marsh grass. This was the river I remembered when I canoed part of the original channel in 1981, vast and windswept. "It feels like we're in Kansas or Nebraska," Julia observed.

"But Julia, we're not in Kansas anymore," I replied. "I see gators."

"Seeing this," said Julia more seriously, "you realize why the channelization of the Kissimmee River was a crime against nature."

We agreed that the restored Kissimmee River will be a great paddling trail and a boon to sportfishermen and bird-watchers. Some primitive campsites have already been set up by the South Florida Water Management District.

Beyond the river floodplain to the northeast lay an area even more reminiscent of the western prairies—the Kissimmee Prairie Preserve State Park. At 54,000 acres, this remote preserve harbors the largest remaining tract of dry prairie in Florida, so it's not surprising that several rare and endangered species such as the Florida grasshopper sparrow, burrowing owl, crested caracara, white-tailed kite, and sandhill crane find refuge there. Also, the park boasts the highest number of butterfly species in one area of Florida—more than eighty-six have been documented.

Fig. 42. Early morning on the Kissimmee River.

On a separate trip, I visited the vast preserve and spoke with manager Charles Brown. "Our first goal is to the restore the land to like it was before white men arrived," he said. "That may mean burning up some shade for hikers." The park service tries to burn half of the preserve every year, mimicking natural lightning fires that once swept the area. Native American hunters and cattlemen also burned the prairie, knowing that the succulent growth that sprouted soon after a fire was favored by grazing animals, and that fire suppressed the tick population. Timber companies, however, objected to the practice since frequent fire knocked back tree growth. In 1879, they convinced the Florida legislature to limit the practice, but the unenforceable law was largely ignored.

In the early 1900s, Texas fever, carried by ticks, killed thousands of Kissimmee valley cattle. Dipping vats for cattle were set up to eradicate ticks, but they proved only marginally effective in some cases. The cattleman George Bronson, in a 1951 interview reprinted in *The River of the Long Water*, recalled the challenge they faced, and the rediscovery of an old ally:

> We lost 800 to 1,000 head of cattle from fever that winter, but finally we got a few dipping vats in operation. We began dipping in 1919, but it didn't do any permanent good. An animal would be cleaned of ticks by dipping, turned back on the range and in three weeks would be loaded with ticks again. Then we began burning the scrub growth on the ranges. That, we discovered, was the source of the reinfestation of cattle which had been cleaned of ticks in the vats, as ticks grew on the underbrush. We cleaned our ranges and our cattle got fat again.

During my visit to the Kissimmee prairie, smoke plumes billowed into a blue sky from a planned fire, and I spotted a herd of deer slowly moving away from the flames, gracefully maneuvering through the sweeping grasslands and low palmetto bushes. As when I gazed upon parts of the restored Kissimmee River, I was caught up in the welcome illusion that little had changed in this part of Florida over millennia.

Fig. 43. A deer roams through sunlit prairie grass at the Kissimmee Prairie Preserve State Park.

Fig. 44. Smoke from a prescribed burn at the Kissimmee Prairie Preserve State Park. Managers try to simulate natural fires that once swept across Florida's largest natural prairie.

Julia and I stopped at Micco Camp, an upland rest stop with a covered shelter and picnic tables. The high ground of this area, part of present-day Micco Bluff, was referenced in the 1882 expedition chronicles:

Here it is that Micco, an Indian chief, celebrated in his tribe for his great bravery and strategy in war, assembled his warriors, determined to make his last stand against the soldiers before taking to the impenetrable fastness of the Everglades. From this point we find, after climbing up the banks, that a perfect view is attained of all the surrounding country. A huge oak stands upon the bank, towering high above all the others. We can see where, many years ago, the limbs were cut off to give an unimpeded view of the surrounding country, and in the body of the tree are the remains of steps cut in the wood to place the feet in when climbing. Taking a field-glass, I climb to the top of the tree, and obtain a perfect view of the whole country through which we have passed that day. The fire we lighted to cook our breakfast was plainly seen in the distance about five or six miles, although we have come at least twenty-five miles by the river. No wonder Micco selected this spot for a lookout, for anyone approaching by water, coming either from the north or south, could be seen plainly for 12 hours before they arrive.

Micco Camp was an ideal tree-canopied setting for Julia and I to meet with a group of teachers who were guided there in a pontoon boat by folks with my agency and the water management district. I love speaking to teachers. If something important sinks in, that lesson can be magnified a hundredfold—year after year with their students. That's how the environmental movement came into being—one person at a time sharing with another until a conservation ethic began to take hold. Julia and I talked about the expedition, our experiences and observations, and the river. Then we left so the teachers could do water-quality experiments with their guides while our main task was to reach our destination before dark.

The Kissimmee is known for its many side channels and oxbows. These were often long river bends that have been abandoned when the river shifted course, leaving an alluring channel that usually leads to a dead-end. The river below Micco Camp had a particularly attractive side channel, lined with lush cypress trees. It lured us in. Since the Kissimmee at this time of year had very little current, it was easy to get confused. We paddled a mile or so before reaching a swampy cove with no outlet. I should have known better since we started going the wrong direction, but with the normal twists and bends of the river, cardinal direction points aren't always reliable. We had to backtrack, losing valuable time.

On this day, like the day before, there was another unknown variable near the end. As the Kissimmee emptied back into the C-38 Canal—the end of the restored section—we approached Lock 65–C. The old river channel cut to the right, but it was blocked, we were told, because the canal had now robbed most of its water flow.

We had three choices on how to proceed. We could paddle to a nearby landing and portage a half mile down a road to the old river channel—beyond the blocked section—that led to the Riverwoods Field Lab, our destination for the night. Or we could try to paddle a tiny canal to the channel leading to the lab, avoiding the long portage. Or, we could paddle the wide C-38 Canal a couple of miles and backtrack a mile or more up the oxbow from the other direction to the lab, adding at least two miles to our day, and taking valuable time. We chose the narrow canal. As we approached it, an old-timer fishing along the shore said the canal ahead was choked with weeds. "But with those boats, you might be able to get through," he said, nodding to our kayaks.

Once on the canal, we realized we were committed. The canal was too narrow to turn around, especially for my boat, which was seventeen feet long. Julia paddled a ten-foot pongo. The old-timer was right; the canal was choked with weeds. We were basically paddling on weeds, pushing off with our paddles. Thick swampland bordered each side. We didn't want to slow our momentum or we might have gotten stuck. After a half mile, the canal opened up, and we spotted a bridge to our left that spanned the old river channel. The problem was that a large metal weir was in our way. A weir either directs or holds back water. We could not move over it with our kayaks, so we had to balance on top of the weir and lift the kayaks over, the water being too deep to wade.

Fortunately, future paddlers will have an easier time of it in this section; they will simply take the winding Kissimmee River since that will be their only choice. Lock 65–C is set to be destroyed, blown up like Lock 65–B. The canal will be filled in and water will no longer be diverted from the old channel. Even the road to the lock will likely be removed. Change was coming.

Once we were on the old channel to Riverwoods, several shallow sections impeded our progress. The old floodplain had been replaced by pastureland; cows grazed along the water. But this section, too, will change in the near future as annual flooding is allowed to return.

We pulled into the Riverwoods Field Lab, tired but happy. It had been another great, tough day. The rest of the group had been wor-

Fig. 45. A red-shouldered hawk eats a snake at Starvation Slough along the restored section of the Kissimmee River.

ried—the hikers came in before us again—so there was relief all around.

The Riverwoods Lab is a former residential neighborhood that was purchased by the water management district as part of the floodplain purchase program. Jointly operated by the district and the Florida Center for Environmental Studies, it supports research and education related to the Kissimmee restoration and the entire Everglades watershed, and it will eventually fall victim to its own success. A few of the buildings that are within the one-hundred-year floodplain will be moved or destroyed as this segment of the river is restored.

Jeff Brooks, owner of the company making the documentary and news spots, greeted us after we set up tents. He was checking on his crew every couple of days, often picking up film to be delivered to Central Florida News 13 for nightly updates about the expedition. "I have a surprise for you guys," he said, smiling. He led us to an old refrigerator freezer in the outdoor kitchen pavilion and opened the door; more than a dozen Ben and Jerry's ice-cream cartons stared back. "Take your pick," he said. With my face still feeling flush from the afternoon sun, I chose Chunky Monkey, trying to keep myself from drooling. I had never eaten an entire cartoon of the rich dessert in one sitting, but I did that night. How do you say weight gain? Despite any challenges we encountered during the day while moving through the Kissimmee system, each evening's camp was a warm and nurturing place of hugs, laughter, and good food. On this night, we had a cookout over a grill.

The next day, after nine straight days of kayaking, I traded my kayak paddle for hiking shoes. Beth and Julia paddled the C-38 Canal against a stiff headwind, while I joined Mike, Doug, Fred, and Ian on the Florida Trail. Our first stop was the Edna Pearce Lockett Estate, a handsome Victorian-era home overlooking the river. Captain John Mizell Pearce built a log cabin on the site in 1875 to serve as a ferry stop for people wanting to cross the river, near the town of Fort Bassinger. Pearce had operated the steamboat *Mary Belle* on the Kissimmee until it sunk. His maximum rates for ferrying people and animals were as follows: Footman (single person on foot), 15¢; man and horse, 25¢; horse and buggy or other single team, 50¢; double team, 75¢; one yoke of oxen and cart or wagon, 40¢; two yoke of oxen and cart or wagon, 60¢; each additional yoke, 15¢; each additional animal, 05¢.

Pearce's granddaughter, Edna Pearce Lockett, was the last tenant of the estate. For several years, Edna Pearce taught in Bassinger's two-room schoolhouse that now sits on the property, but after her father's death in 1944, she became the sole manager of the family's ranching operations and was dubbed "the one-woman ranch." She was only the third woman ever to be elected to the Florida House of Representatives, where she fought for women's rights and succeeded in securing funding to pave U.S. 98 from Fort Bassinger to Sebring and passing a law that required Florida beef to be accurately labeled. While she did push through a law that allowed women to serve on juries—at their request—she was unsuccessful in convincing the male-dominated legislature to abolish discriminatory wage rates based on sex.

Serving for three terms, Lockett joked that she had to get elected to get anything done in her area. She married the English wool importer William James Lockett in 1953 and retired from politics. "She was a fabulous role model for women," concluded Louisa Kerwin, director of the Riverwoods Field Lab.

During her induction into the Florida Agricultural Hall of Fame in 1998, a few years after her death, Lockett was commemorated for being "as comfortable on a ranch chatting with a Cracker cowboy as she was working the halls of the Legislature."

After Lockett's death, her trust donated the 35-acre property and historic homestead to the South Florida Water Management District as part of the land acquisition for the restoration project. But the district doesn't see managing a historical site as part of its mission, so it offered the county a half million dollars to take it since the large house needed renovation. The county was cool to the idea. Florida Atlantic University also refused the offer, and so did the Florida Trail Association. When Fred Davis told us about the situation—the home without a home—I joked to him, "Heck, I'll take it for a half million dollars!"

A group that would love to have the estate remain in public ownership is the Highlands County Historical Preservation Commission. The day before, representatives of the commission visited us to talk about the estate. "When you are there, you really feel like you can hear the heart of Florida beating," said Katherine Cornelius. The preservation commission has plans to make the historic landmark a working farm with docents in period costume, but first ownership and management of the estate have to be settled.

After touring the property and agreeing that it had tremendous educational potential, we said our good-byes to Fred, who was heading home. We crossed a bridge to the east side of the river—no more need for a ferry—and began hiking the Florida Trail through parched cattle country, dipping in and out of live oak groves. The land seemed thirsty, and though we didn't know it at the time, that spring marked the beginning of central and south Florida's worst drought since record keeping began in 1932. Lake Okeechobee receded to an all-time low, and uses of water such as watering lawns were severely restricted. Only the conditions creating the 1930s Dust Bowl were considered worse.

To end the day, we hiked along a blistering highway for six miles, the only shade being from an occasional lone palm tree. I yearned for the cool waters of the Kissimmee. I hoped that in the future the Florida Trail Association could buy a wooded corridor in this stretch.

Back at camp after fifteen miles of walking, I had sore feet, legs, and hips to go along with my sore arms, shoulders, and back. Beth mercifully offered to rub my feet in exchange for a massage of her shoulders. I planned to paddle the remainder of the trip, but at least I was an official "hiyaker."

The camera crew had their own adventure. After the stop at the Edna Pearce Lockett Estate, they somehow got turned around on the wrong side of the river, drove down a road that they thought led to the campsite, and ended up at a ranch with a sign that proclaimed: "Warning! Trespassers Will Be Shot and Eaten."

"So we took pictures of that and the huge dogs barking at us," Virginia said.

Our camp that night was closed in by barbed wire to keep out cows; we were surrounded by semi-wooded cattle country. Mosquitoes were thick. The only other hum was from a small generator for the film crew as they reviewed footage in their large tent. A few of us decided to walk to the canal for the sunset and visit with Steve, the tender for Lock 65–D for the past two years. He pointed out where a new floodgate was being built to handle excess water from the restoration. The kayakers, he said, were the first nonmotorized watercraft to pass through the lock.

Living in a nearby house overlooking the reflective waters of the canal, Steve vowed to never leave "until they throw my ashes off the lock." It always amazes me how people can develop that kind of strong attachment to a body of water, even a heavily altered one such as a canal or reservoir. Water has a way of capturing us. Maybe since water is the dominant element in our own bodies, we are drawn to it like kindred spirits.

Since it was April 1, April Fool's Day, we decided to take advantage of the annual opportunity to play practical jokes. We devised a plan. Upon returning to camp, I called Matt, our main coordinator in Tallahassee, who hadn't been able to join the expedition. I acted upset, then hung up as if the cell phone disconnected. We waited a few minutes, knowing Matt would be gripped with worry. Virginia then called Matt. With a convincing urgency in her voice, she began a tale of woe, "Matt, the hikers are all upset and mutinying," she said. "They haven't shown up at the campsite. I think they hitchhiked to a motel somewhere and are quitting the expedition!"

Virginia held up the phone so we could hear his response, "That doesn't sound good at all!" After taking a second to catch his breath, he asked, "What about the kayakers? Have they arrived?"

"Yes, but they refuse to talk to me. I think they know where the hikers are, but they won't divulge the information. I think the whole expedition is breaking up."

Matt's voice broke a bit. "I, I'm not sure what I can do from up here at this point." He sounded helpless.

We couldn't let him suffer any more. On the count of three, we yelled, "April Fool's!"

"I'm sorry Matt, they made me do it!" Virginia chimed in.

We could hear Matt sigh. "I need to go the bathroom and wash the word 'sucker' off my forehead," he said good-naturedly.

"We love ya, man!" we called out before hanging up. For those left behind, it's important to include them in the fun whenever possible.

To top off the evening, Jeff Brooks showed up again with more Ben and Jerry's ice cream. Did he have stock in the company? I downed

Fig. 46. Julia Thompson on Telex Marsh along the old channel of the Kissimmee River.

another quart, Chubby Hubby, I think. Health food for the trail. At home, my wife, Cyndi, had trimmed down with Weight Watchers. Any desserts in the house had one or two grams of fat per serving. I had clearly fallen "off the wagon." I felt as though I was eighteen years old again, thru-hiking the Appalachian Trail. I had lost weight on that journey while being a ravenous eating machine, but an eighteen-year-old body metabolizes food differently than a fifty-year-old one. When I returned home from the expedition, I would trip the scales three pounds heavier. Upper body muscle, I maintained, and that's the story I'm sticking with.

The next day, on a dead-calm morning, Julia and I paddled a meandering section of the original river channel. Fish popped, turtles ducked, and we surprised two black-crowned night herons. Sabal palms reflected on the dark glassy water.

Near the Telex Marsh Landing, the river character changed completely. High banks and moss-laden live oaks were reminiscent of the Upper Suwannee. The river seemed to beg for restoration. Once in the canal again, we made our way to the Kissimmee River Fishing Resort to celebrate our last night on the journey. Shingle Creek seemed a long way away, but some of its water was here, only a few miles from Lake Okeechobee.

The "resort" itself seemed less geared for fishing than a home for winter and year-round residents. Large recreational vehicles and trailers were packed tightly together. Many appeared to have been parked there for years, with mailboxes, sheds, and colorful signs stating family names, the kind you would find in a residential neighborhood. It was typical of many of south Florida's dusty RV parks and trailer parks, where scores of seniors on fixed incomes have sacrificed spaciousness for balmy winter weather. Not all who migrate to the "Sunshine State" can afford beachside condos or gated golf course communities. The one demographic commonality is that the sun worshippers are generally from north of the Mason-Dixon Line. Southern accents are rare.

Walking up from our kayaks to the resort's grassy tent area spread under arching live oak trees, we were greeted by a smiling young woman with the words "Massage Therapist" emblazoned on her T-shirt. "I'm Tracy, and I'm here to give anyone a massage who wants one," she said. Jeff Brooks, our "trail angel," had hired her. She had a massage table set up under the live oaks. So, while resort residents in golf carts cruised on the road around our open campsite, craning their necks to see what was happening since we were likely the most fascinating exhibit to have come along in quite some time, Tracy relaxed our sore muscles. How many long-distance hikers or paddlers are treated to such luxury near the end of their journeys? Jeff showed up with pizza and beer, and we gave him a standing ovation.

Since this was our last night, several team members wrote conclusionary remarks on a Department of Environmental Protection blog via a satellite computer. "I have seen the wealth of Florida on this expedition," wrote Mike Jones. "Not hotels and condos, but woods, water and all that inhabit them. I have also seen the ones who care and watch over it all for the future. They are professional and dedicated."

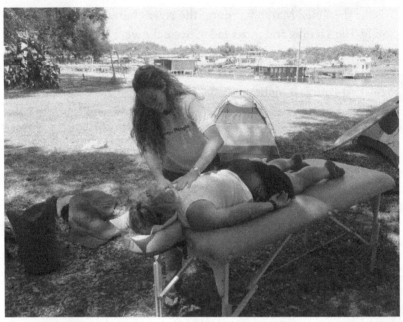

Fig. 47. Massage therapist Tracy Vinson massages Julia Thompson at the Kissimmee River Fishing Resort, the group's last campsite.

Ian Brown added: "Let's make a difference in what we do by seeing beyond the simple decision of what costs less today and see how we can live a more sustainable life now for the future of our people. Conserve water, waste less, and consume less."

Beth Kelso: "A good friend told me one time that a great journey is enjoyed in three ways: planning the trip, experiencing the trip, and then reliving the trip by sharing your experiences with others. I can truly say that this expedition to the heart of Florida has been an extraordinary experience in every way."

Julia Thompson added, "A highlight for me was seeing the 'Real Florida.'"

The expedition was ending too soon for most of us. A week and a half had zipped by, and if we had turned around and headed north at that point, we likely would have been surprised at what we had missed the first time through. Our experience was only as wide as our vision, and with changes in weather, circumstances, and the people and wildlife we encountered, the whole experience could be different. Wild Florida can be as multifaceted as you want to make it.

chapter 11

~~~~~~~~~~~~~~~~~~~~~

Blue Horizon

We embarked soon after first light for our last day. Julia and I passed through the final lock of the trip, one that bore the original name of 65–E. Then we met a smiling man paddling upriver to meet us. Bob had left a downriver launch area before dawn and watched the sun slowly break over the horizon while on the water. "I've been watching an otter along the shore," he said. "I took some great photos."

The last few miles down a stretch called Paradise Run were bittersweet; we knew the trip was ending. Passing a large housing development along the western shore of the canal didn't lift our spirits any. This part of the Kissimmee will likely never be restored. "Hey, you guys want some coffee or something," a man yelled from his manicured backyard. "I've been watching your progress on the news!" We politely refused his kind offer; "civilization" had come too abruptly. The winding Kissimmee and wild shores of the chain of lakes were now behind us. By dark, we would be sleeping on a real mattress inside four walls and wondering why the night was so quiet.

The alligators left the best for last. At the river's mouth, nearly all of the scaly beasts that cruised in from shore to greet us were at least ten feet long. I was glad the winds were calm so there was little chance of capsizing.

As we paddled into Lake Okeechobee, an oceanlike expanse of freshwater that is second in size only to Lake Michigan in the continental United States, blue water stretched across the horizon. Even though its perimeter has been diked for flood control and the level

Fig. 48. An otter romps along the Kissimmee River in the early morning on the expedition's last day. Photo by Bob Mindick.

and flow of water through it is heavily manipulated, the huge lake is still a magnificent water body.

To the south, across the vast blue lake, are agricultural lands and then the famed "river of grass," a shallow 100-mile-long swath of sawgrass marsh, tree islands, and slow-moving water that most people associate with the Everglades. I briefly imagined the challenges and beauty associated with paddling that stretch and ending at Florida Bay. Only in high water could it possibly be done.

Okeechobee is often referred to as Florida's liquid heart, pumping life-giving freshwater to south Florida's people, farms, and natural environments. It has also brought death and destruction.

Originally, Okeechobee's southern shore spilled into a massive swamp. Water spread out to feed the remainder of the Everglades system, but with drainage projects creating dry land beginning in the late 1800s, agriculture moved in. The naturalist Charles Torrey Simpson, on an expedition to the lake in 1917 with John Kunkel Small, remarked on the disappearing pond apple hammocks and other plant communities that once thrived along the lake's southern rim.

> All the glamour and mystery which once surrounded the great lake, all the wildness and loneliness, . . . its peace and holiness are fast disappearing before the advance of the white man's civilization and soon it will be only a sheet of dirty water surrounded by truck gardens and having winter homes on the eastern shore. . . . It should have been preserved as a state or government reservation where its rare flora and rich wild fauna, its mystery and beauty could have been kept forever.

To protect the emerging farms and towns, a small mud dike was built around the lake to hold back water. Enter the hurricane of September 1928. Lake water was already high from heavy August rains, and the category 4 or 5 storm burst open the dike. A wall of mud and water eleven feet high swept across farms and towns, drowning people and livestock.

Fig. 49. Entering Lake Okeechobee on the last day of the expedition.

Vernie Boots was fourteen years old when the storm hit. About sixty people, including Boots and his family, packed a neighbor's sturdy house near Belle Glade. Like a war veteran gripped with grief, even six decades later, Boots emotionally described what happened when the dike broke in an interview with Jeff Klinkenberg in 1992:

> As it came into the house, everybody moved to the attic. I was one of the last into the attic. . . . The house kept shifting, and a window broke, and the glass cut a piece out of my hand. . . . The house became buoyant. . . . Floated off the foundations.
>
> We floated over to where the government had been building a road. The wind smashed the house against the road bed. We rocked badly and smashed into the road bed again. The third time we hit the road the house fell apart. The last thing my mother said was, "Whatever happens, stay together."

A piece of ceiling became his life raft, and Boots found himself alone in a terrifying sea of churning water and black sky.

> The wind liked to have turned me over. The big thing I tried to do is keep my head pointing at the wind. That and keeping my balance. I kept rotating on that thing, keeping my balance all night. It was dark, real dark, except for lightning. I mean, you couldn't see nothing. The wind was a constant screech. Finally, about daylight, the wind started to die. I yelled for help. Two of my brothers answered. We'd been real close during the night but we hadn't seen or heard each other. They'd been hanging to other pieces of wood, too.
>
> Nothing was left of the community where I lived except for four palm trees. Whatever you was wearing is what you had. . . . They found the bodies of my father and brother—they're buried in a cemetery near the Caloosahatchee River—but my mother was never found. I never saw my mother again.

Almost two thousand people perished during the 1928 hurricane—one of the country's most devastating natural disasters—prompting the government to begin a thirty-year project of building a massive dike. At 150 miles long, 150 feet wide, and towering up to 45 feet, the Hoover Dike encircles the entire lake. The engineering feat enabled more swamp to be drained, enhancing what became known as the nation's winter vegetable basket—the more than 700,000-acre Everglades Agricultural Area.

But the benefits to the country's food supply and the enhanced storm protection came at a price; water flow into the southern Everglades was diminished and became increasingly polluted with pesticides and phosphorous. The Everglades was in trouble, along with the thousands of animals that depended upon it. Enter Marjory Stoneman Douglas. The release of her *Everglades River of Grass* in 1947 coincided with the establishment of Everglades National Park. Awareness began to seep in that the Everglades was beneficial to animals and people in a natural state, not merely as land to be drained, developed, or farmed. Douglas and many others fought ongoing attempts to destroy the unique ecosystem, and they began a long uphill battle to restore what had already been impaired.

"No matter how poor my eyes are I can still talk," Douglas said in her 1987 autobiography. "I'll talk about the Everglades at the drop of a hat. Whoever wants me to talk, I'll come over and tell them about the necessity of preserving the Everglades. Sometimes, I tell them more than they wanted to know."

Frail and nearly blind at the end, Douglas never stopped fighting for the Everglades. She fought death with the same tenacity, finally succumbing in 1998 at age 108.

Nat Reed, former assistant secretary of the interior and former board member of South Florida Water Management District, said this about Douglas soon after her death:

What Marjory clearly saw and understood long before other competent observers was that the sugar business was not only wreaking environmental havoc, but causing political problems as well. Lake Okeechobee was being destroyed by the back-pumping of billions of gallons of highly nutrified discharge, and south Florida's water supplies were being artfully directed by staff of the water management district to benefit Big Sugar and the winter crop growers in south Dade County.

Most of the environmental community felt that some compromise would have to be made. Not Marjory! She traveled to

Clewiston, the heart of "sugarland." She told the corporate leadership that it was not only their water and air pollution, their excessive demands for water supply and drainage, and their unique ability to avoid paying their fair share of costs associated with maintaining the water management system that caused problems. Even worse was their corporate power to influence Florida lawmakers, thus solidifying her resolve to urge cessation of sugar farming and to return the southern portion of the Everglades agricultural area to marsh.

At the time, I felt that Marjory had gone too far. But years later, having served fourteen years on the South Florida Water Management District, I am convinced that Marjory was right. Sugar production in Florida has made for incredible wealth among a small group of investors and, in my opinion, is the cause of political influence that is being misused.

Two years after Douglas's death, Congress passed the nearly $11 billion Comprehensive Everglades Restoration Plan (CERP). If successful, the world's most famous wetlands will slowly return to some of its former glory, reviving habitat for nearly seventy threatened and endangered species. The plan, funded 50–50 by the state and federal governments, is part restoration and part water supply since numerous farms and millions of people along the east and west coasts of Florida now depend upon the freshwater that the Everglades provides. Vast surface reservoirs and numerous underground storage wells will be built to hold water during the wet season so it will be available during dry times, better enabling managers to time water deliveries to mimic natural patterns. The majority of water that now goes out to sea will be redirected into the Everglades. About 240 miles of canals and levees will be removed to allow for better sheet flow—the spreading out of water over wide marshlands. Polluted runoff from farms and urban areas will continue to be abated with marsh-filtering systems and other means. Development is being redirected away from the Everglades in places such as Miami-Dade County.

Successes along the Kissimmee River will serve as a model and inspiration for the broader plan, but the challenges are great. More than half of the original Everglades wetlands have been lost to encroaching cities, subdivisions, and farms. In restoring the Kissimmee, mostly undeveloped cattle land was purchased; trying to restore an ecosystem bordered by human development and intensive agricultural operations is an altogether different and more complex matter. Plus, there are the effects of climate change to anticipate as sea levels rise and coastal marshes migrate inland. One hope is that improved freshwater flow through the entire system will help to create a freshwater barrier that will keep rising seas at bay, slowing ecosystem changes so animals and plants—and people—can better adapt.

There are lingering questions and doubts about the CERP, however. Anglers, for example, are concerned about losing recreational access if certain canals are filled. But the injection of up to a billion gallons of water per day into a series of more than three hundred deep wells— a key component of the plan known as Aquifer Storage and Recovery (ASR)—has drawn the most attention. Army Corps of Engineers scientists believe that the freshwater will float on top of the heavier brackish water in a type of underground bubble, allowing it to be recovered as needed. This will help to eliminate surface evaporation so that water will be available when it is most needed.

Critics such as Mark Perry, a marine scientist and director of the Florida Oceanographic Society, maintain that ASR is too theoretical and that the plan itself is overly engineered. "Congress voted to restore the Everglades," he said, "but when you get into the details, most of the projects are construction projects. Too much emphasis is being placed on flood protection, drainage, and water supply for agriculture and urban residents. The restoration of the south Florida ecosystem, while mentioned in the plan, takes a back seat."

Perry, the Sierra Club, and groups such as the one Douglas founded, Friends of the Everglades, have long argued that restoration money would be better spent on purchasing farmland in the Everglades Agricultural Area and restoring sheet flow south of Lake Okeechobee.

Proponents concede that the Everglades plan is not a purist doctrine. It was passed only after years of intense deal-making between powerful, diametrically opposed interest groups such as Big Sugar and Audubon of Florida. Bob Dawson, representing various Florida industries, lobbied for the plan in Congress. Soon after passage, he concluded, "If it was just an environmental plan, it never would have gotten out of the bog."

Environmental groups that lobbied in favor of the plan claim they can be more effective working on the inside. "If I were the emperor of the world, I would do the plan differently," said Mark Kraus of Audubon of Florida soon after the bill passed, "but the fact is that we have over 6 million people living in south Florida right now, and we have to deal with that. There are sixty-eight major projects, and each will need their own plans. While we support the conceptual plan, we are playing close attention to the individual components as they are developed."

Kraus said that Audubon supports ASR but urged the Corps to move quickly to a contingency plan in case it fails. He also emphasized the need to identify and purchase private lands that are required before land is developed or prices go up. "Otherwise, it could spiral out of control," he said.

One aspect of the plan that wildlife biologists are studying closely are the effects on upland tree islands within the Everglades since these are the oases for deer, panther, and a host of other land animals, and they are used by wading birds, snail kites, and reptiles for nesting. The islands are threatened by either excessive flooding or by extreme drawdowns that can leave them vulnerable to fire. Scheduling water releases that follow a more natural rainfall-driven schedule is the key to reducing these extremes.

The timing of water flows is also key to the survival of Florida's largest estuary—Florida Bay—situated at the bottom of the Everglades. Because the hydrology of the Everglades system has been severely altered by canals, development, and farms, Florida Bay has been starved of vital freshwater—a 70 percent decline, by one estimate. It is, for the most part, too salty, and freshwater often flows in at the wrong time of year. Many of its native life forms have suffered. Seagrass die-offs, algae blooms, and fish kills blemish its recent past. Seasonal rains bring temporary relief, but the long-term hope lies squarely with the Comprehensive Everglades Restoration Plan.

"Historically, more water was held back by vegetation in the Everglades in what is known as dynamic storage," said Bill Perry, an ecologist with Everglades National Park. "The sheet flow would trickle freshwater into the bay over time. You need good water depth in the upstream marshes during the wet season so that water can continue trickling into the bay late into the dry season. Now, with less Everglades and less water in the remaining Everglades, the coastal marshes begin drying out in November and December instead of January and February."

The nesting season for roseate spoonbills and other wading birds is in March and April. Historically, fish would be concentrated in shrinking coastal ponds and streams during this time of year, enabling parent birds to easily scoop up fish to feed their young. For years, however, water managers released water into the bay during spring in order to keep urban and agricultural areas dry. Fish were dispersed into a much broader area. That's devastating for nesting spoonbills, according to Jerry Lorenz, the director of research for Audubon of Florida.

"Everybody loves to see spoonbills," said Lorenz. "They're probably the most photogenic bird around. They're on the covers of many books and magazines, and yet they're doing horribly, and nobody seems to want to 'fess up to the problem. The spoonbill is the best ecological indicator for how freshwater hits Florida Bay."

Spoonbill numbers in Florida Bay have dropped by more than half since 1980, and by 90 percent at the mouth of Taylor Slough, one of the bay's major feeder streams. The year 2008 was the worst one yet for spoonbills in Florida Bay. Only 292 nests were identified during the nesting season, a 37 percent drop from the previous year. A key solution will be to improve the timing and quantity of water inflows into the bay. If Lorenz is correct, success will be measured by the number of brilliant "flame birds" dotting the mangrove shorelines of Florida Bay.

As the Everglades plan moves forward, rising fuel costs and land prices have escalated the total cost, but state and federal officials are still confident it will succeed. "There are technological solutions to all the possible problems," said Peter Kwiatkowski, the lead project manager for the South Florida Water Management District. "I don't see anything as being a deal breaker."

Most parties agree that the alternative to CERP—doing nothing—would bring about the continued demise of the Everglades and Florida Bay.

The mix of restoration options was expanded in June 2008, when Governor Charlie Crist proposed the buyout of the United States Sugar Corporation's land holdings south of Lake Okeechobee for an estimated $1.75 billion. The purchase of an area more than twice the size of Orlando, 187,000 acres, would end the massive amounts of phosphorous, nitrogen, and other chemicals that U.S. Sugar annually pumped onto their sugarcane fields. These fertilizers ended up in Everglades wetlands and caused excessive plant growth and decay and a reduction in water quality, otherwise known as eutrophication, or the dirty water was back-pumped into Lake Okeechobee. The buyout will also allow huge amounts of water to be stored during the wet seasons—up to 1.2 cubic kilometers—instead of being drained seaward to prevent flooding.

While sugar-loving farm towns such as Clewiston were chagrined at hearing the news, Everglades activists felt they had won the environmental lottery. "The significance of this cannot be overstated," said Everglades Foundation senior scientist Dr. Tom Van Lent. "It will allow us to eliminate about 85 percent of the damaging releases to the St. Lucie and Caloosahatchee, and it will do so decades earlier than we thought possible."

Some predict that the controversial Aquifer Storage and Recovery (ASR) component of the Everglades plan may be reduced or scrapped as a result of the purchase. "With this landmark acquisition, we now have the ability to make better decisions about how to complete the restoration plan," said Mark Perry of the Florida Oceanographic Society.

Crist had come up with the buyout proposal during a meeting with sugar lobbyists the previous November. The lobbyists were complaining that if the company were no longer allowed to back-pump polluted water into Lake Okeechobee, a way of removing excess water from their fields, it would severely hamper their business. "I have an idea. Why don't we just buy you out?" Crist reportedly said. And so the discussions began.

The day after Governor Crist's dramatic announcement, Nat Reed praised him in a letter. "Marjory Stoneman Douglas, shortly before her death, bedeviled by the inaction of the board and staff of the South

Florida Water Management District to make meaningful changes in the operation of the Everglades Agricultural Area, announced that the only solution was 'to buy them out!' Marjory is looking down on you with a smile on her face."

Paddling into Lake Okeechobee, which has traditionally served as a natural reservoir for the southern Everglades, I wondered what has kept the vision of a restored Kissimmee River and Everglades alive. Perhaps the vision is sustained by the places that still exist in the Everglades system—beyond canals, farms, and sprawl—where one can slosh or paddle and still feel a wild pulse. Alligators, wading birds, snail kites, and bald eagles continue to feed, mate, and soar. And somewhere in the vastness, the elusive Florida panther roams an ancestral territory.

Some of the native people who still live along the sawgrass, the Seminole and Miccosukee, say that it is their traditional songs and dances that have kept the system alive, and that their lawsuits forcing government agencies to clean up the water haven't hurt either. But I also like to think that the animals, plants, trees, and many other life forms that make up the wild pulse of the system are not altogether powerless. Maybe they have a say in their fate? After all, they've been around a lot longer than we have—and they may outlive us all.

Not long before her death, Marjorie Stoneman Douglas wrote, "Perhaps even in this last hour, in a new revelation of usefulness and beauty, the vast, magnificent, subtle and unique region of the Everglades may not be utterly lost." If the Kissimmee River is any indication, those words may prove prophetic.

We rounded a point and landed in black muck at the Okie-Tantie Recreation Area. The hikers raced out to greet us. Soon, we were splashing and having a muck fight, like students celebrating the last day of school. "Let's get the anchorwoman!" Ian shouted.

Virginia had waded out to document the moment along with her crew, videographer Jeff Cook, and sound mixer Josh Harris. Virginia shrieked as she got soaked and muddied, while Jeff and Josh recorded it for posterity. "It took me twenty minutes to get all the muck off me," she said afterward, laughing.

We had a short ceremony, and Matt brought low-fat foods to share

Fig. 50. Expedition members on the last day after a mud fight along the shores of Lake Okeechobee.

such as pizza and thickly frosted cake. The expedition was over. But I knew that the lakes and waterways of the Kissimmee valley had cast a spell not easily shaken. It has lured many to explore, exploit, and reconcile our past. Now it is teaching us to love a place without killing it.

Epilogue

A few months after the expedition, I visited the Rosen Shingle Creek Resort in Orlando for a meeting of the Everglades Working Group. The goal of the diverse coalition of government and private representatives is to expand passive recreation opportunities in the Kissimmee valley, including the establishment of a 140-mile paddling trail. I also had a personal motive for attending. I wanted to see my hat.

You see, at the postexpedition celebration along Lake Okeechobee, I had all of the expedition team members and support people sign my white broad-rimmed Tilly hat with a permanent marker. Then, a few weeks later, I presented it to Harris Rosen in appreciation for his support of the expedition. He said he would display it in his new A Land Remembered Steakhouse once it opened. The restaurant was named for Patrick Smith's classic Florida novel about the Kissimmee cattle country, *A Land Remembered*. Rosen is a big fan of the book. Now that the steakhouse was open, I walked over with high anticipation.

A sharply dressed host greeted me. When I explained my purpose, and that I wasn't interested in ordering the New York strip, he smiled and guided me to the glassed-in wine pantry. There, amidst the elaborate temperature-controlled collection of multicolored bottles, was my hat for all to see. It hung on a hook with a sign attached that described the expedition. My old friend was still as sweat-stained and mildewed as I remembered. That hat had shielded my head from sun and rain on several kayaking and canoeing expeditions, from north Florida's spring-fed rivers to nearly all parts of the Florida coast and to its last journey, down the Kissimmee valley. It had history, that hat, and I was proud to see it. It seemed appropriate that it rested here, at the headwaters of the Everglades.

Perhaps the hat and what it symbolized will inspire others to paddle the Kissimmee valley as we did. The opportunities will only get better with time. Adjoining counties have been purchasing land for passive recreation along the trail corridor, and the Trust for Public Land is seeking help from the private sector to fill in gaps. Eventually, more campsites will be developed throughout the system as an alternative to the sometimes noisy fish camps. Discussions have ranged from finding suitable land on high ground to building elevated camping platforms above the flood zone.

Once the Kissimmee River restoration is complete, more campsites will likely be established along the restored sections of river, and paddlers will not have to contend with construction zones. One fewer lock and dam will need to be navigated, too.

The best way to keep up with the ongoing progress of land purchases and river restoration is to log onto the Web sites of Orange, Osceola, Polk, Okeechobee, Highlands, and Glades counties and the South Florida Water Management District. Also, the Florida Department of Environmental Protection has a comprehensive Web site on the Everglades restoration, and the Florida Trail Association sells detailed maps for its established hiking trail along the Kissimmee River (check Internet search engines for these easily found sites since Web addresses can change over time). The water management district also has a handy recreation guide that features campsites, launches, and recreational opportunities for the lands and waters they manage. Eventually, a trail guide for the entire Kissimmee valley will likely be developed.

Owing to the immense size of some of the lakes along the route, a fully equipped sea kayak is recommended as winds and storms can create choppy, oceanlike conditions. Canoes would be suitable for the Kissimmee River portion of the route. Most of the fish camps along the system feature small stores for resupply, along with potable water. The middle portion of the Kissimmee River has few available amenities, so a water purifier and adequate food supplies are recommended.

The main requirement for a Kissimmee valley journey is a sense of adventure and a yearning for what wild Florida has to offer.

Bibliography

Akerman, Joe A., Jr. *Florida Cowman: A History of Florida Cattle Raising*. Kissimmee: Florida Cattlemen's Association, 1976.

Alberson, Sarah D. "King of the Crackers." 1953. Reprint, *Florida Wildlife*, November–December 2003, 28–30.

Alderson, Doug. "Everglades Restoration: Can We Pass the Test?" *Florida Wildlife*, January–February 2002, 2–3.

———. "The Florida Trail." *Florida Wildlife*, March–April 2003, 2–5.

———. "The Many Moods of Florida Bay." *Florida Wildlife*, January–February 2003, 2–5.

———. "New Dawn for the Kissimmee?" *Geojourney*, April 1981, 4–8.

Asfar, Dan. *Ghost Stories of Florida*. Auburn, Wash.: Lone Pine, 2005.

Barnett, Cynthia. "Final Frontier: Growth Is Coming to Florida's Heartland." *Florida Trend*, July 2006, 48–53.

Cantrell, Elizabeth A. *When Kissimmee Was Young*. Kissimmee: First Christian Church, 1948.

"Celebration Homes for Sale." www.homes.com/Real_Estate/FL/City/CELEBRATION.

Crow, Myrtle Hilliard. *Old Tales and Trails of Florida*. Kissimmee: Osceola County Historical Society, 1987.

Dean, Cornelia. "The Preservation Predicament." *New York Times*, January 29, 2008.

Derr, Mark. *Some Kind of Paradise: A Chronicle of Man and the Land in Florida*. New York: William Morrow, 1989.

"Disney Development's Newest Project: Celebration, Florida." Celebration Realty fact sheet. http://celebration.nm1.net/.

Douglas, Marjory Stoneman. *The Everglades: River of Grass*. 1947. Covington, Ga.: Mockingbird Books, 1974.

Douglas, Marjory Stoneman, with John Rothchild. *Voice of the River*. Sarasota: Pineapple Press, 1987.

Everglades Coalition. "Everglades Coalition Supports Historic Buyout." Press release, June 30, 2008.

Everglades Foundation. "Everglades Foundation: Massive Land Acquisition Is 'Priceless, Breathtaking Opportunity to Save Fabled River of Grass.'" Press release, June 24, 2008.

Florida Agricultural Hall of Fame. "Edna Pearce Lockett." www.flaghalloffame.com/inductees/1998/1998.html.

Florida Department of Agriculture and Consumer Services. "Lightsey Cattle Company." www.florida-agriculture.com/news/lightsey_cattle.htm.

Florida Department of Environmental Protection. "Everglades Forever: Why Restore the Everglades and Lake Okeechobee?" www.dep.state.fl.us/evergladesforever/restoration/default.htm.

———. "Florida Completes 100,000 Acre Land Acquisition for Kissimmee River Restoration." Press release, April 11, 2006.

———. "How Was Hydrilla Introduced into Florida?" Bureau of Invasive Plant Management Circular 18. http://iswgfla.org/files/Circular18.pdf.

Florida's Invasive Species Working Group. "Channeled Apple Snails." www.iswgfla.org/Channeled%20applesnails.htm.

Gergis, Nadia. "New Kind of Master Plan Communities Being Built for the Boomers." Panama Investor Blog, May 6, 2006. http://primapanama.blogs.com/_panama_residential_devel/2006/05/new_kind_of_mat.html.

Gratton, Melora. "Testing to Commence for Controversial Everglades ASR System." www.enviro-net.com/main.asp?page=story&id=7&month=07&paper=fl&year=2004.

Grunwald, Michael. "Swamp Thing: The Plan to Restore the Everglades Is Not What You Think It Is." *Slate*, June 15, 2001. http://www.slate.com/id/110378/.

———. *The Swamp: The Everglades, Florida, and the Politics of Paradise*. New York: Simon and Schuster, 2006.

Hancock, Ruby Jane. "The Kissimmee Valley: An Appreciation." *Tequesta* 39 (1979): 17–28.

Hetherington, Alma. *The River of the Long Water*. Chuluota, Fla.: Mickler House, 1980.

Huffstodt, James. "Yesterday's Dream." *Florida Wildlife*, July–August 1994, 22–23.

Hundley, Kris. "Yeehaw's Destiny Awaits." *St. Petersburg Times*, June 4, 2006. www.sptimes.com/2006/06/04/Business/Yeehaw_s_Destiny_awai.shtml.

Kam, Dara. "Historic Deal Was 7 Months in Making." *Palm Beach Post*, June 24, 2008.

King, Robert P. "Reservoir Cost May Top $700 Million." *Palm Beach Post*, February 1, 2008.

———. "Roseate Spoonbill Suffering May Be a Sign of Everglades Woes." *Palm Beach Post*, March 5, 2008.

Klinkenberg, Jeff. *Dispatches from the Land of Flowers*. Asheboro, N.C.: Down Home Press, 1996.

Levin, Ted. *Liquid Land: A Journey through the Florida Everglades*. Athens: University of Georgia Press, 2003.

Mahon, John K. *History of the Second Seminole War 1835–1842*. 1967. Rev. ed. Gainesville: University Presses of Florida, 1985.

Marshall, Arthur R., Jr. "For the Future of Florida Repair the Everglades." 3rd ed., 1982. Friends of the Everglades Digital Library. http://everglades.fiu.edu/marshall/FI06011102/index.htm.

McCally, David. *The Everglades: An Environmental History*. Gainesville: University Press of Florida, 1999.

McIver, Stuart B. *Dreamers, Schemers and Scalawags: The Florida Chronicles, Volume 1*. Sarasota: Pineapple Press, 1994.

Mills, Bubba. "The Great Valley." 1982. Friends of the Everglades Digital Library. http://everglades.fiu.edu/marshall/FI06011102/index.htm.

Missall, John, and Mary Lou Missall. *The Seminole Wars: America's Longest Conflict*. Gainesville: University Press of Florida, 2004.

Molloy, Johnny. *Hiking the Florida Trail*. Gainesville: University Press of Florida, 2008.

Mueller, Edward A. "Kissimmee Steamboating." *Tequesta* 26 (1966): 53–87.

Palmer, Tom. "2 Planned Toll Roads Would Cross Polk." *Bartow Ledger*, April 14, 2006. www.theledger.com/apps/pbcs.dll/article?AID=/20060414/NEWS/604140381&SearchID=73247945398110.

Pinnell, Gary. "Commissioners Seem Cool to Lockett Estate." *Highlands Breaking News*. www.tboblogs.com/index.php/community/comments/commissioners-seem-cool-to-lockett-estate.

Preble, George Henry. "A Canoe Expedition into the Everglades in 1842." *United Service: A Quarterly Review of Military and Naval Affairs* (April 1883): 358–76. Reprint, *Tequesta* 5 (1945): 30–51.

Reed, Nathaniel Pryor. "Memories of Marjory Stoneman Douglas and Her Everglades Crusade." *Foresight* (Fall 1998). www.1000friendsofflorida.org/natural/Marjory_Stoneman_Douglas.asp.

———, to Governor Charlie Crist. June 25, 2008.

Remington, Frederic. "Cracker Cowboys of Florida." *Harper's*, August 1895, 339–45.

Robison, Jim. *Kissimmee: Gateway to the Kissimmee Valley*. Charleston: Arcadia, 2003.

"Roseate Spoonbill." National Audubon Society Web site. http://web1.audubon.org/waterbirds/species.php?speciesCode=rosspo.

Rothra, Elizabeth Ogren. *Florida's Pioneer Naturalist: The Life of Charles Torrey Simpson*. Gainesville: University Press of Florida, 1995.

Sashin, Daphne. "13,000-Home Plan for Osceola Clears First Hurdle," February 21, 2008. www.orlandosentinel.com/news/local/osceola/orl-locosc-growth21022108feb21,0,883166.story.

"Seminole Tribe Buys Hard Rock Café Business." December 8, 2006. www.msnbc.msn.com/id/16090321/.

Smith, Patrick D. *A Land Remembered*. Sarasota: Pineapple Press, 1984.

South Florida Water Management District. *Recreational Guide*. West Palm Beach, 2007.

Ste. Claire, Dana. *Cracker: The Cracker Culture in Florida History*. Daytona Beach: Museum of Arts and Sciences, 1998.

Stowe, Harriet Beecher. *Palmetto Leaves*. Boston: J. F. Osgood, 1873. Reprint, with new introduction. Gainesville: University Press of Florida, 1999.

Tinsley, Jim Bob. *Florida Cow Hunter: The Life and Times of Bone Mizell*. Gainesville: University Press of Florida, 1990.

Van Landingham, Kyle. *Pioneer Families of the Kissimmee Valley*. 1976. www.lamartin.com/history/pearce_family.htm.

Van Sickler, Michael, and Shannon Colavecchio-Van Sickler. "Heartland Parkway Receives Cool Reception from Governor." *St. Petersburg Times*, March 6, 2007. http://evergladesfoundation.net/article2.php?id=19.

United States Army Corps of Engineers and the South Florida Water Management District. "About the Comprehensive Everglades Restoration Plan." www.evergladesplan.org/index.aspx.

United States Fish and Wildlife Service. "Slowing the Spread of the Island Channeled Apple Snails." Conference notes, 2006. www.fws.gov/florida-panther/exotics/exotics_notes2006.html.

Wall, Steve, and Harvey Arden. *Wisdomkeepers: Meetings with Native American Spiritual Elders*. Hillsboro, Ore.: Beyond Worlds, 1990.

Whitney, Ellie, D. Bruce Means, and Anne Rudloe. *Priceless Florida: Natural Ecosystems and Native Species*. Sarasota: Pineapple Press, 2004.

Will, Lawrence E. *Okeechobee Boats and Skippers*. St. Petersburg: Great Outdoors, 1964.

Williams, Archie P. "Across South Central Florida in 1882." *New Orleans Times-Democrat*, December 3, 1882. Reprint, *Tequesta* 10 (1950): 49–88.

Williams, Lindsey, and U. S. Cleveland. *Our Fascinating Past: Charlotte Harbor*,

The Early Years. Punta Gorda: Charlotte Harbor Area Historical Society, 1993.

Interviews

Brown, Charles. Riverwoods Field Lab. 2008.
Kern, Jim. Telephone conversation. 2003.
Koebel, Joseph. Riverwoods Field Lab. 2008.
Kraus, Mark. Telephone conversation. 2001.
Lightsey, Cary. Brahma Island. 2007.
Lorenz, Jerry. Telephone conversation. 2002.
Mann, Marty. Lake Tohopekaliga. 2001.
McCoy, Doug. Telephone conversation. 2003.
Perry, Bill. Telephone conversation. 2002.
Perry, Mark. Telephone conversation. 2001.
Rosen, Harris. Rosen Shingle Creek Resort. 2007.
Royce, Ray, and Steve Royce. Lake Istokpoga. 2001.

Index

Page numbers in italics refer to illustrations.

Florida Crackers, 16–17, 103
Florida Department of Community Affairs, 73
Florida Department of Environmental Protection, 1, 123, 138
Florida Department of Transportation, 73
Florida Fish and Wildlife Conservation Commission, 19, 31
Florida Forever, 37
Florida Heartland, 71
Florida House of Representatives, 119
Florida Keys, 11
Florida Oceanographic Society, 131, 134
Florida Panhandle, 88–89, 91
Florida panther, 6–7, 40–41, 135
Florida Trail, 3, 50; description of, 88–92; and Kissimmee River section, 97, 107, *109*, 109, 120
Florida Trail Association, 1, 3, 98, 119, 138; history of, 89–90
Florida Wildlife, 16, 37
Florida Wildlife Federation, 81
Fort Bassinger, 94; town of, 118–19
Fort Christmas, 16
Fort Gardner, 94
Fort Kissimmee, 94
Fort Meade, 65
Fort Myers, 106
Friends of the Everglades, 76, 83, 131

Geojourney, 81
Georgia, 64, 71
Ghost Stories of Florida (Asfar), 108
Glacier National Park, 10
Graf, Bill, 31, 57–58
Graham, Bob, 84–85
Great Smoky Mountains National Park, 8
Guido, Bob, 20
Gulf of Mexico, 11, 53, 81
Gulf of St. Lawrence, 91

Hancock, Ruby Jane, 69
Harmony (Fla.), 71
Harper's, 68
Harris, Josh, 135
Hatch, Nettie Bass, 7–8
Hatchineha, Lake, 30, *42*, 43–44, 94
Hattaway, Doug, 3, 91, 97, 118
Hawk, red-shouldered, *117*

Heartland Coast-to-Coast, 72–74
Heartland Parkway, 72–74
Hendry, Capt. Francis Asbury, 65–66
Hetherington, Alma, 108
Highlands County Historical Preservation Commission, 119–20
Hike for Hope, 91
Hiking the Florida Trail (Molloy), 90
Hilliard's Island, 16
History of the Second Seminole War (Mahon), 94–95
Hock, Gary, 20
Hollywood (Fla.), 96
Hoover Dike, 128
Hunter's Creek Middle School, 5, 5–6
Hurricane of 1928, 127–28
Hydrilla (Indian starvine), 19–20

Ibis, glossy, 54; white, *79*
Immokolee, 38
Istokpoga, Lake, 37–43
Istokpoga Canal, 37
Itasca, Lake, 53

Jacksonville, 29
Jernigan, Isaac, 14–15
Jim, Buffalo, 25
Johns, Mary, 96
Johnson, Virginia, 19, 60, *62*, 93, 120–21, 135
Jones, Johnny, 81, 84
Jones, Mike, 3, 31, 60, 91, 123; and hiking Kissimmee Valley, *49*, 97, 118; and paddling Kissimmee River, 98–110, *100*
Jumper, 94

Katahdin, Mount, 91
Kelso, Beth, 3, 13, 31, 58, 120, 124; and hiking Kissimmee valley, *49*, 91, 97; and paddling Kissimmee River, 118
Kern, Jim, 88–90
Kerwin, Louisa, 119
Key West, 91
Kicco, 88–89
Kissimmee: and cattle ranching, 68; early history of, 6–9, 14–15, 106; flooding of, 25, 80; and flooding prevention, 36
Kissimmee: Gateway to the Kissimmee Valley (Robison), 65, 105

ing paddle, 52; paddling Lake Kissimmee, 52, 54, 58, 76; protesting camping fees, 57

Minnesota, 53

Mississippi River, 5

Mizell, David, 17

Mizell, Morgan Bonaparte Bone, 66–67

Molloy, Johnny, 90

Morris, Rick, 101

Mueller, Edward A., 106

Muskogee Creek Indians, 51

New Orleans Times-Democrat, 28, 44, 102

New urbanism, 71

New York City, 29, 97

Ocala National Forest, 89

Office of Greenways and Trails, 1, 5

Ohio River Valley, 106

Okeechobee, Lake, 1, 6, 11, 50, 62, 96, 123, *127*, 137; backpumping into, 129, 134; building of dikes around, 127–29; description of, 125–27; drought effects on, 120; effects of Kissimmee River channelization on, 80–81; effects of weather patterns on, 83; hurricane effects on, 127–28; trail along dikes of, 90

Okeechobee County, 9

Okeechobee (Fla.), 70, 90

Okie-Tantie Recreation Area, 135

Oklahoma Territory, 95

Old Tales and Trails of Florida (Crow), 7–9, 15–16

O'Neal, Shaquille, 60

Opa-Locka, 48

Orlando, 1, 4, 11, 17, 90; early history of, 9, 16, 69; pollution from, 6, 31

Osceola County, 21, 24, 66, 71

Osceola County Historical Society, 16

Osceola County Parks, 1, 3

Osceola, Max, 97

Osceola National Forest, 89

Osprey, *55*

Overstreet, E.L.D., 7

Owl, burrowing, 111

Oxfam America, 91

Palm Beach, 17

Palmetto Leaves (Stowe) 102

Paradise Island, 14, 20–21

Paradise Run, 125

Parker, Polly (Ma-de-lo-yee), 96

Patrick, Hannigan, 9

Pearce, John Mizell, 118

Pelham, Tom, 73–74

Perry, Bill, 132–33

Perry, Mark, 131, 134

Philip, King, 12

Preble, George Henry: describing natural passages between Kissimmee chain of lakes, 35; grave robbing by, 35; hardships endured by, 35–36; wild foods described by, 34; wildlife described by, 18

Pugliese, Anthony V., III, 72

Punta Gorda, 67–68

Punta Rassa, 67–68

Reagan Administration, 85

Red wolf, 8

Reed, Nat, 129–30, 134–35

Reedy creek, 31, 33–34

Remington, Frederic, 68

Renney, Jerry, *47*, 47–48

Residents Organized Against Restoration (ROAR), 85

Rezolution Productions, 3

Riddick, Ayounga, 1, 30–31, 98

River of the Long Water, The (Hetherington), 108, 113

River otter, *126*

Riverwoods Field Lab, 116, 118–19

Robison, Jim, 65, 105

Rodgers, John, 75

Roseate spoonbill, 29, *30*, 133

Rosen, Harris, *4*, 4–5, 137

Rosen Shingle Creek Resort, 1, 4–5, 137

Rothchild, John, 83

Royce, Ray, Jr., 37–39

Royce, Steve, 37–39

Russell, Lake, 31

St. Augustine, 65

St. Cloud, 8

St. Johns River, 102

St. Lucie River, 134

St. Marks, 96

Doug Alderson, of Tallahassee, is the author of numerous magazine articles and three books. His first book, *Waters Less Traveled: Exploring Florida's Big Bend Coast* (2005), was the North American Travel Journalists Association runner-up for Best Travel Book of 2006. He is the Florida Paddling Trails coordinator for the Florida Department of Environmental Protection's Office of Greenways and Trails. To learn more, log on to: www.dougalderson.net.